ons in association with Neil McPherson
rough Theatre presents

duction in more than 50 years

ATION ON A THEME

ce Rattigan

FINBOROUGH | THEATRE

First perfo   1958.
First perfo   2014.

D0412157

zappshot
Audition Technology

Zappshot is a revolutionary new audition technology, designed to simplify the screen audition process from the minute you step into the casting studio.

Zappshot can be used by **casting directors**, **producers**, **directors**, **production companies** and **actors**. You will experience an easy-to-use, fast and reliable system that will benefit all parties.

"Zappshot will make the entire screen audition process smoother, easier, faster and more user friendly."

To find out more please visit

www.zappshot.com

VARIATION ON A THEME

by Terence Rattigan

Cast in order of speaking

Hettie	**Susan Tracy**
Rose	**Rachael Stirling**
Ron	**Martin McCreadie**
Kurt	**Phil Cheadle**
Fiona	**Rebecca Birch**
Mona	**Emma Amos**
Adrian	**Jamie Coleman**
Sam	**David Shelley**

The action takes place on the terrace of a villa in the South of France, 1958.

The performance lasts approximately two hours and fifteen minutes.

There will be one interval of fifteen minutes.

Director	**Michael Oakley**
Designer	**Fotini Dimou**
Lighting Designer	**Matt Eagland**
Sound Designer	**Max Pappenheim**
Assistant Director	**Charlie Parham**
Assistant Designer	**Pippa Scarcliffe**
Production Manager	**George Hughes**
Costume Supervisor	**Adrian Lillie**
Props Supervisor	**Lisa Buckley**
Music Supervisor	**Steve Edis**
Ballet Consultant	**Charlotte Toner**
Company Stage Manager	**James Theobold**
Assistant Stage Manager	**Jamie Coleman**
Press Representative	**Lewis Jenkins for The Cornershop**
Print Design	**June Frangue**
Production Image	**Edward Quinn**
Producers and General Management	**Sarah Hammond, Ben Prudhoe** and **Sam Zdzieblo** for HPZ Productions

Emma Amos | Mona
Theatre includes *66 Books Writer Neil La Bute* (Bush Theatre), *Hay Fever* (West Yorkshire Playhouse), *Accidental Death of an Anarchist* (Donmar Warehouse), *The Servant* (Lyric Hammersmith), *Gracenote* (Old Vic Theatre), *Sweet Bird of Youth, The Birthday Party* (National Theatre) and *Apples* (Royal Court Theatre).

Films include *Mother's Milk, Blackball, Vera Drake, Bridget Jones's Diary, The Tribe, Firelight, Secrets and Lies, Buddy's Song, A Ghost in Monte Carlo* and *Rowing with the Wind*.

Television includes *Holby City, Silent Witness, Poirot, My Family, Heartbeat, The Bill, The Golden Hour, The Last Detective, Midsomer Murders, Alistair McGowan's Big Impression, Goodnight Sweetheart* and *Moving Story*.

Rebecca Birch | Fiona
Theatre includes *Relative Values* (Theatre Royal Bath), *Health Wealth* (Old Vic New Voices), *Pygmalion* (Chichester Festival Theatre and Garrick Theatre) and *The Master Builder* (Chichester Festival Theatre).

Films include *Long Forgotten Fields, D-Effects, The Lost Boy* and *Welcome to Leathermill*.

Workshops include *The Life and Times of Fanny Hill* (Bristol Old Vic) and *The Ruby Necklace* (Charing Cross Theatre).

Phil Cheadle | Kurt
Productions at the Finborough Theatre include *Events While Guarding the Bofors Gun*. Trained at RADA.
Theatre includes *Blue Remembered Hills* (Northern Stage), *Neighbourhood Watch*, *Dear Uncle* (Stephen Joseph Theatre, Scarborough), *Bedlam*, *Henry IV Parts 1 and 2* (Shakespeare's Globe), *Knives and Hens*, *Tartuffe* (Arcola Theatre), *All My Sons* (Curve Theatre, Leicester), *Mrs Affleck* (National Theatre), *Far From the Madding Crowd* (English Touring Theatre), *If I Were You* (Library Theatre, Manchester), *The Tempest*, *Saint Joan* (A and B C Theatre Tour), *Macbeth* (West Yorkshire Playhouse), *The Changeling* (Cheek by Jowl), *A Midsummer's Night Dream* (Creation Theatre), *Strawberry Fields* (Pentabus) and *As You Like It* (Northcott Theatre, Exeter).
Films include *John Carter of Mars*, *Comes a Bright Day* and *A Touch of Sadness*.
Television includes *The Ark*, *New Worlds*, *Inside the Titanic*, *Coronation Street* and *Inspector Lynley*.

Jamie Coleman | Adrian
Trained at the Arts Educational Schools.
Theatre includes *An Ideal Husband* (St James Theatre Studio).

Martin McCreadie | Ron

Martin is the winner of Best Actor at the 2011 Edinburgh Fringe Festival for his portrayal of Alex DeLarge in *A Clockwork Orange* (Soho Theatre and Australia Tour).

Theatre includes *Romeo and Juliet* (Camden People's Theatre), *Dostoyevsky's Notes from Underground* (Etcetera Theatre), *Bold and Brave Festival* (Cockpit Theatre), *Titus Andronicus* (Space Theatre), *Trainspotting, The Long and the Short and the Tall* (Playhouse Theatre) and *Frankenstein* (Frantic Assembly).

Short films include *On the Edge of Town*, *Reel Lives* and *Tread Softly*.

David Shelley | Sam

Trained at LAMDA.

Theatre includes *Happiness* (King's Head Theatre), *Betrayal* (Gala Theatre, Durham), *The Country, Copenhagen* (Tabard Theatre), *Cider with Rosie* (New Vic Theatre, Stoke), *Hobson's Choice* (Theatre Royal York), *Julius Caesar, Romeo and Juliet* (Royal Shakespeare Company), *As You Like It, Antony and Cleopatra* (English Shakespeare Company) and *Three Steps to Heaven* (Palace Theatre, Watford).

Films include *Fast Girls*.

Television includes *The White Queen, The Politician's Husband, EastEnders, Doctors, Hollyoaks, Holby City, Casualty, Red Cap, The Bill, Ultraviolet*, Catherine Cookson's *The Round Tower, Bramwell* and *Rough Treatment*.

Rachael Stirling | Rose

Rachael has been twice nominated for an Olivier Award.

Theatre includes *Medea* (National tour), *The Recruiting Officer* (Donmar Warehouse), *An Ideal Husband* (Vaudeville Theatre), *A Midsummer Night's Dream* (Rose Theatre, Kingston), *The Priory* (Royal Court Theatre), *Pygmalion* (Theatre Royal Bath and Japan), *Uncle Vanya* (Wilton's Music Hall), *Look Back in Anger* (Theatre Royal Bath), *Tamburlaine* (Bristol Old Vic) and *Theatre of Blood* (National Theatre).

Films include *Sixteen*, *Snow White and the Huntsman*, *Salmon Fishing in the Yemen*, *The Young Victoria*, *The Triumph of Love*, *Complicity*, and *Still Crazy*.

Television includes *The Game*, *The Bletchley Circle*, *Doctor Who*, *Boy Meets Girl*, *Tipping the Velvet*, *Women in Love*, *Riot at the Rite*, *The Haunted Airman* and *Othello*.

Susan Tracy | Hettie

Susan has been twice nominated for an Olivier Award.

Theatre includes *Rattigan's Nijinsky*, *The Deep Blue Sea* (Chichester Festival Theatre), *The Relapse*, *Three Sisters*, *Anna Christie*, *Merry Wives of Windsor*, *Othello* (Royal Shakespeare Company), *Much Ado About Nothing* (Open Air Theatre, Regent's Park), *Long Day's Journey into Night* (Cambridge Theatre Company), *The Old Wives' Tale* (New Victoria Theatre, Stoke), *Denial* (Bristol Old Vic), *Anything Goes* (National Theatre and Theatre Royal Drury Lane), *A Passage to India* (Shared Experience, national tour and BAM in New York), *Richard II*,

Inherit the Wind (The Old Vic), *Playhouse Creatures* (Chichester Festival Theatre) and *A Chorus of Disapproval* (Harold Pinter Theatre).
Television includes *Midsomer Murders, The Stars Look Down, Born and Bred, The Diary of Anne Frank* and *Poirot*.

Terence Rattigan | Playwright
Rattigan was born in South Kensington, close to the Finborough Theatre, in 1911. His many classic plays include *French Without Tears, After The Dance, Flare Path, While The Sun Shines, The Winslow Boy, The Browning Version, Harlequinade, The Deep Blue Sea, The Sleeping Prince, Separate Tables, Variation On A Theme, Ross, Man And Boy, A Bequest To The Nation, In Praise Of Love* and *Cause Célèbre*. He also wrote screenplays for such classic films as *The Way To The Stars, Journey Together, While the Sun Shines, The Winslow Boy, The Browning Version, The Prince And The Showgirl, Separate Tables, The Sound Barrier, The Deep Blue Sea, The VIPs, The Yellow Rolls Royce* and collaborated on *The Quiet Wedding, The Day Will Dawn* and *Brighton Rock*. His television plays include *Heart To Heart, Adventure Story* and *High Summer*. He was awarded a CBE in 1958, and knighted in 1971. Sir Terence Rattigan died in 1977. Please visit the official Terence Rattigan website at www.terencerattigan.co.uk

Michael Oakley | Director
Michael is a recipient of the JMK Award for Young Directors for which he directed *Edward II* at BAC. In 2012 he was Co-Artistic Director of Chichester Festival Theatre's pop-up space Theatre on the Fly. Direction includes *Playhouse Creatures* (Chichester Festival Theatre), *The Changeling* (Southwark Playhouse), *Shooting Truth* (NT Connections)

and *Graceland* (The 24 Hour Plays: Old Vic New
Voices). Associate Direction includes *Relative Values*
(Theatre Royal Bath and national tour), *Kiss Me
Kate* (The Old Vic), *The King's Speech* (West End
and national tour), *Rosencrantz and Guildenstern
Are Dead* (Chichester Festival Theatre and West
End). Assistant Direction includes *Inherit The
Wind* (The Old Vic), *A Month in the Country*, *The
Critic* and *The Real Inspector Hound*, *Oklahoma!*,
Cyrano de Bergerac (Chichester Festival Theatre),
tHe dYsFUnCKshOnalZ! (Bush Theatre) and *Much
Ado About Nothing* (Globe Education). Michael was
trainee director-in-residence at Chichester Festival
Theatre and has also completed a training course
with Cheek by Jowl.

Fotini Dimou | Designer
Trained in Fine Art in Brussels before studying
Theatre Design at the Central St Martins School of
Art and Design.
Theatre includes *The Duchess of Malfi*, *The Castle*, *A
Jovial Crew*, *The School of Night*, *The Archbishop's
Ceiling*, *Ion*, *Fashion*, *The Storm*, *Speculators*
(Royal Shakespeare Company at Stratford-upon-
Avon and Barbican Theatre), *Sore Throats*, *Road*,
Some Singing Blood, *The Queen and I* (Royal
Court Theatre), *Romeo and Juliet* (Victory Theatre,
Broadway) and costumes for *Creditors* (Donmar
Warehouse and Brooklyn Academy of Music, New
York), *The Girl with the Pearl Earring* (National
Tour and Theatre Royal Haymarket), *Hay Fever*
(Chichester Festival Theatre), *Romeo and Juliet*,
Twelfth Night (Open Air Theatre, Regent's Park),
The Last Confession (Chichester Festival Theatre
and Theatre Royal Haymarket), *Present Laughter*
(Royal Exchange Theatre, Manchester), *Madame*

Melville (Vaudeville Theatre), *Saturday, Sunday, Monday* (Chichester Festival Theatre), *Julius Caesar* (Royal Shakespeare Company at Stratford-upon-Avon and the Roundhouse), *The Crucible, Principia Scriptoriae* (Royal Shakespeare Company at Stratford-upon-Avon and the Pit) and *The Changeling* (Southwark Playhouse). She has also designed sets and costumes for ballet, modern dance, opera as well as costumes for feature films and television including *The Browning Version, Ripley's Game* and *Skin*.

Fotini's recent work includes three new dance pieces for Richard Alston's Dance Company at the Barbican Theatre. Forthcoming work includes costume design for *Manon Lescaut* (Baden-Baden Opera) directed by Sir Richard Eyre and costumes for the international tour of *The Last Confession*, starring David Suchet and directed by Jonathan Church.

Matt Eagland | Lighting Designer
Matthew trained at the Guildhall School of Music and Drama, before eventually heading the lighting departments of both the Yvonne Arnaud Theatre, Guildford, and Cambridge Arts Theatre. He has subsequently designed the lighting for many productions throughout the UK and internationally.

Recent theatre includes *It's a Wonderful Life* (Pitlochry Festival Theatre), *Kindertransport, September in the Rain, Mansfield Park* (National Tours), *Intimate Exchanges* (The Mercury Theatre, Colchester) and *Flow* (The Print Room).

Other theatre includes Derren Brown's *Svengali* (National Tour and Palace Theatre), *The West End Men* (Vaudeville Theatre), *Cool Hand Luke* (Aldwych Theatre), *Broken Glass* (Vaudeville Theatre), *The Secret of Sherlock Holmes, Little Women* (Duchess

Theatre), *Carrie's War* (Apollo Theatre, Shaftesbury Avenue), *Terre Haute* (New York), *Darwin in Malibu* (Birmingham Rep), *Moon on a Rainbow Shawl*, *Our Man in Havana* (Nottingham Playhouse), *Haunting Julia, My Boy Jack, An Hour and a Half Late* (National tours), and *Copenhagen* (Watford Palace Theatre). Opera includes *I Lombardi* (UC Opera London), *La Traviata, L Elisir di Amore* (English Touring Opera), *La Finta Semplice, Jacko's Hour, The Long Christmas Dinner, The Dinner Engagement* (Guildhall School of Music and Drama), *L'Heure Espagnol* and *Gianni Schicchi* (Opera Scotland).

Max Pappenheim | Sound Designer
Productions at the Finborough Theatre include sound design and composition for *Black Jesus, Summer Day's Dream, The Hospital at the Time of the Revolution, Somersaults, The Soft of Her Palm* and *The Fear of Breathing* and directing *Nothing is the End of the World (Except for the End of the World)* (nominated for three OffWestEnd Awards), and *Perchance to Dream*.
Other sound design includes *Fiji Land, Our Ajax* (Southwark Playhouse), *Mrs Lowry and Son* (Trafalgar Studios), *CommonWealth* (Almeida Theatre), *Being Tommy Cooper* (Yvonne Arnaud Theatre, Guildford and National Tour), *The Mystery of Irma Vep, Borderland, Kafka v Kafka* (Brockley Jack Studio Theatre), *Four Corners One Heart* (Theatre503), *Word:Play NWxSW* (Octagon Theatre, Bolton, and National Tour for Box Of Tricks), *Freefall* (New Wimbledon Theatre Studio), *Below the Belt* (Edinburgh Festival). As Associate Designer, *The Island* (Young Vic). Max was nominated for an OffWestEnd Award 2012 for Best Sound Designer.

Special Thanks to

John Brant, Alan Brodie of Alan Brodie Representation, Adrian Brown, Amelia Ferrand-Rook and Katie Hennessey at Chichester Festival Theatre, Gavin Kalin of Totally Theatre Productions, David King at St Gabriel's Pimlico, Neil Laidlaw, Barbara Longford of The Terence Rattigan Society, Michael McCabe, Playful Productions, David Stone and Michael Watt.

Our patrons are respectfully reminded that, in this intimate theatre, any noise such as rustling programmes, talking or the ringing of mobile phones may distract the actors and your fellow audience-members.

We regret there is no admittance or re-admittance to the auditorium whilst the performance is in progress.

FINBOROUGH | THEATRE

VIBRANT **NEW WRITING** | UNIQUE **REDISCOVERIES**

"Audacious and successful...West London's Finborough Theatre is one of the best in the entire world. Its programme of new writing and obscure rediscoveries remains 'jaw-droppingly good'". *Time Out*

"A disproportionately valuable component of the London theatre ecology. Its programme combines new writing and revivals, in selections intelligent and audacious." *Financial Times*

"The tiny but mighty Finborough...one of the best batting averages of any London company" Ben Brantley, *The New York Times*

"The Finborough Theatre, under the artistic direction of Neil McPherson, has been earning a place on the must-visit list with its eclectic, smartly curated slate of new works and neglected masterpieces" *Vogue*

Founded in 1980, the multi-award-winning Finborough Theatre presents plays and music theatre, concentrated exclusively on vibrant new writing and unique rediscoveries from the 19th and 20th centuries. Behind the scenes, we continue to discover and develop a new generation of theatre makers – through our literary team, and our programmes for both interns and Resident Assistant Directors.

Despite remaining completely unsubsidised, the Finborough Theatre has an unparalleled track record of attracting the finest creative talent who go on to become leading voices in British theatre. Under Artistic Director Neil McPherson, it has discovered some of the UK's most exciting new playwrights including Laura Wade, James Graham, Mike Bartlett, Sarah Grochala, Jack Thorne, Simon Vinnicombe, Alexandra Wood, Al Smith, Nicholas de Jongh and Anders Lustgarten; and directors including Blanche McIntyre.

Artists working at the theatre in the 1980s included Clive Barker, Rory Bremner, Nica Burns, Kathy Burke, Ken Campbell, Jane Horrocks and Claire Dowie. In the 1990s, the Finborough Theatre first became known for new writing including Naomi Wallace's first play *The War Boys*; Rachel Weisz in David Farr's *Neville Southall's Washbag*; four plays by Anthony Neilson including *Penetrator* and *The Censor*, both of which transferred to the Royal Court Theatre; and new plays by Richard Bean, Lucinda Coxon, David Eldridge, Tony Marchant and Mark Ravenhill. New writing development included the premieres of modern classics such as Mark Ravenhill's *Shopping and F***king*, Conor McPherson's *This Lime Tree Bower*, Naomi Wallace's *Slaughter City* and Martin McDonagh's *The Pillowman*.

Since 2000, new British plays have included Laura Wade's London debut *Young Emma*, commissioned for the Finborough Theatre; two one-woman shows by Miranda Hart; James Graham's *Albert's Boy* with Victor Spinetti; Sarah Grochala's *S27*; Peter Nichols' *Lingua Franca*, which transferred Off-Broadway; and West End transfers for Joy Wilkinson's *Fair*; Nicholas de Jongh's *Plague Over England*; and Jack Thorne's *Fanny and Faggot*. The late Miriam Karlin made her last stage appearance in *Many*

Roads to Paradise in 2008. We have also produced our annual festival of new writing – *Vibrant – A Festival of Finborough Playwrights* annually since 2009.

UK premieres of foreign plays have included plays by Brad Fraser, Lanford Wilson, Larry Kramer, Tennessee William, the English premiere of Robert McLellan's Scots language classic, *Jamie the Saxt*; and three West End transfers – Frank McGuinness' *Gates of Gold* with William Gaunt and John Bennett; Joe DiPietro's *F***ing Men*; and Craig Higginson's *Dream of the Dog* with Dame Janet Suzman.

Rediscoveries of neglected work – most commissioned by the Finborough Theatre – have included the first London revivals of Rolf Hochhuth's *Soldiers* and *The Representative*; both parts of Keith Dewhurst's *Lark Rise to Candleford*; *The Women's War*, an evening of original suffragette plays; *Etta Jenks* with Clarke Peters and Daniela Nardini; Noël Coward's first play, *The Rat Trap*; Charles Wood's *Jingo* with Susannah Harker; Emlyn Williams' *Accolade*; Lennox Robinson's *Drama at Inish* with Celia Imrie and Paul O'Grady; John Van Druten's *London Wall* which transferred to St James' Theatre; and J. B. Priestley's *Cornelius*, which transferred to a sell out Off-Broadway run in New York City.

Music theatre has included the new (premieres from Grant Olding, Charles Miller, Michael John LaChuisa, Adam Guettel, Andrew Lippa, Paul Scott Goodman, and Adam Gwon's *Ordinary Days* which transferred to the West End) and the old (the UK premiere of Rodgers and Hammerstein's *State Fair* which also transferred to the West End), and the acclaimed 'Celebrating British Music Theatre' series, reviving forgotten British musicals.

The Finborough Theatre won The Stage Fringe Theatre of the Year Award in 2011, *London Theatre Reviews'* Empty Space Peter Brook Award in 2010 and 2012, the Empty

Space Peter Brook Award's Dan Crawford Pub Theatre Award in 2005 and 2008, the Empty Space Peter Brook Mark Marvin Award in 2004, and swept the board with eight awards at the 2012 OffWestEnd Awards including Best Artistic Director and Best Director for the second year running. *Accolade* was named Best Fringe Show of 2011 by *Time Out*. It is the only unsubsidised theatre ever to be awarded the Pearson Playwriting Award (now the Channel 4 Playwrights Scheme) nine times. Three bursary holders (Laura Wade, James Graham and Anders Lustgarten) have also won the Catherine Johnson Award for Pearson Best Play.

www.finboroughtheatre.co.uk

FINBOROUGH | THEATRE

The Finborough Theatre has the support of the Channel 4 Playwrights' Scheme, sponsored by Channel 4 Television and supported by The Peggy Ramsay Foundation.

The Finborough Theatre is a member of the Independent Theatre Council, the Society of Independent Theatres, Musical Theatre Network, The Friends of Brompton Cemetery and The Earl's Court Society www.earlscourtsociety.org.uk

Mailing
Email admin@finboroughtheatre.co.uk or give your details to our Box Office staff to join our free email list. If you would like to be sent a free season leaflet every three months, just include your postal address and postcode.

Follow Us Online

www.facebook.com/FinboroughTheatre
www.twitter.com/finborough

Feedback
We welcome your comments, complaints and suggestions. Write to Finborough Theatre, 118 Finborough Road, London SW10 9ED or email us at admin@finboroughtheatre.co.uk

Playscripts
Many of the Finborough Theatre's plays have been published and are on sale from our website.

Finborough Theatre T Shirts
Finborough Theatre T Shirts are now on sale from the Box Office, available in Small, Medium and Large £7.00.

Smoking is not permitted in the auditorium and the use of cameras and recording equipment is strictly prohibited.

In accordance with the requirements of the Royal Borough of Kensington and Chelsea:
1. The public may leave at the end of the performance by all doors and such doors must at that time be kept open.
2. All gangways, corridors, staircases and external passageways intended for exit shall be left entirely free from obstruction whether permanent or temporary.
3. Persons shall not be permitted to stand or sit in any of the gangways intercepting the seating or to sit in any of the other gangways.

THE TERENCE RATTIGAN SOCIETY

President: Princess George Galitzine, MBE
Vice Presidents: Michael Darlow. Greta Scacchi.
David Suchet, CBE. Geoffrey Wansell.
Chairman: Barbara Longford

The Terence Rattigan Society was founded in 2011, one of many events that year celebrating the centenary of the birth of the playwright widely recognised as perhaps Britain's greatest Twentieth Century dramatist – Terence Rattigan. The Society exists to promote, study, explore, but above all, enjoy Rattigan's work.

Terence Mervyn Rattigan (June 10th 1911 – November 30th, 1977) was born in London, the son of the troubled marriage of a British diplomat and an Edwardian beauty. His passion for the theatre was ignited early when, aged six, he was taken to a performance of *Cinderella*. He began writing plays while still at school and enjoyed his first success in 1933 while at Trinity College, Oxford, when a play, written with a fellow undergraduate, was produced in London. A serious comedy depicting the loose lives and loves of a group of Oxford undergraduates, *First Episode*, caused a minor scandal and was briefly transferred to the West End. Emboldened by this early taste of success, Rattigan left Oxford without taking a degree to embark on a career as a playwright. His father, although disappointed by his son's decision, agreed to pay him a small allowance to live at home and write plays for the next two years on condition that if, after two years, he had not succeeded as a playwright he would accept whatever job his father could find for him.

In the next two years Rattigan wrote six plays, but in vain – none was produced. With the two years up, Rattigan took up a post, found for him by his father, as a junior member of the team of hack screen-writers employed by Warner Brothers at Teddington Studios.

Rattigan's fortunes changed dramatically in November 1936 when a previously rejected comedy, *French Without Tears*, about students studying at a crammers in France, was put on as a cheap stopgap at the Criterion Theatre. It became an unexpected smash hit, running for over 1,000 performances and turning its author and young, little known cast – which included Rex Harrison, Roland Culver and Trevor Howard – into stars. This sudden change in fortune triggered what Rattigan later described as a nervous breakdown. During the next six years he completed only one full length play – *After the Dance* (1939), a powerful drama about failure, loss of ideals and unequal love. It received good reviews but, owing to the outbreak of World War Two, closed after just 60 performances.

Advised by a psychiatrist to enlist for active service, Rattigan joined the R.A.F. as an Air Gunner/Wireless Operator and flew missions with Coastal Command. This experience ushered in the most successful and productive period of his career. In just twelve years he produced ten plays, including *Flare Path* (1942), *While the Sun Shines* (1943) – which ran for over 1,000 performances – *The Winslow Boy* (1946), *The Browning Version* (1948), *The Deep Blue Sea* (1952) and *Separate Tables* (1954), plus screenplays for more than a dozen films.

However, the arrival of a new, younger generation of actors and writers in the 1950s – the success of Samuel Becket's *Waiting For Godot*, the first visit to London of Bertolt Brecht's Berliner Ensemble and, above all, the opening of John Osborne's *Look Back In Anger* in May 1956 – made Rattigan and his contemporaries appear old fashioned. This impression was heightened by Rattigan himself who wrote articles and gave ill-advised press interviews belittling the new theatrical generation and their work. Out of favour with the critics, Rattigan seemed to lose heart. But then in the summer of 1957 he began work on a new play, a re-working of Alexandre Dumas' *La Dame Aux Camelias*. Rattigan intended *Variation On A Theme* as a riposte to the exaggerated criticism to which he and playwrights of his generation had be subjected. He told journalists his new play would 'blow up the establishment' and that people would be shocked by 'the frankness of its theme'. Based in part on the tempestuous relationship of his favourite actress, Margaret Leighton, with the unscrupulous, young, bisexual actor Laurence Harvey, at heart *Variation On A Theme* probed many of Rattigan's own deepest feelings and emotional relationships. Unfortunately, given a bad production by John Gielgud and in the face of the prevailing, generally hostile, attitudes towards Rattigan, the play received a critical hammering out of all proportion to any faults in the play itself. Although fearlessly defended by the distinguished critic T.C. Worsley and a small band of dedicated Rattigan supporters, the play closed after only 132 performances. It has not received a full scale professional production since.

Deeply discouraged, Rattigan devoted much of the rest of his life to writing highly paid film scripts. Nevertheless, during this final period of his career he did produce three of his finest plays – *Man and Boy* (1963), *In Praise of Love* (1973) and *Cause Célèbre* (1977).

By his death, in 1977, Rattigan's reputation was again on the rise and as time passed the number and frequency of revivals of his work grew. In 2010, in the run-up to the centenary of his birth, the National Theatre staged a superb production of *After The Dance* and in 2011, the centenary year itself, there were outstanding London revivals of, among others, *Flare Path*, *Cause Célèbre* and *The Browning Version* at Chichester. The centenary also saw the "world premiere" of a 'lost' 1944 play *Less Than Kind*, a stage adaptation of his unproduced TV play Nijinsky, a well-received rehearsed reading at the Minerva

Theatre, Chichester of *Variation On A Theme*, plus a range of exhibitions, cinema retrospectives and other Rattigan events. In 2013 there were major new productions of The Winslow Boy at The Old Vic in London and in New York and the first professional production of Rattigan and John Gielgud's never professionally staged 1935 adaptation of Dickens' *A Tale of Two Cities*.

Variation On A Theme has been out of print for many years. So this new edition of the play, together with a production at London's award-winning Finborough Theatre in 2014, should offer Rattigan's many modern admirers an opportunity to assess for themselves whether it should, indeed, be numbered as amongst his finest works.

Today Rattigan is widely regarded as the English Chekhov. His plays, while firmly rooted in the times in which they were written, remain as true and emotionally engaging as at the time of their composition. Their characters remain as real and their problems as deeply moving, the plays' themes and the issues of fundamental principle and morality with which they deal as relevant, and the comedies as hilariously funny as ever.

Membership of The Terence Rattigan Society offers members a regular magazine with articles by leading playwrights, biographers and critics, theatre listings, news and views. There are theatre visits at discount prices and trips to places associated with Rattigan – his birthplace, his home at Albany, his schools, etc. plus exhibitions, master-classes and a range of other events associated with Rattigan. But perhaps the greatest benefit of membership is the opportunity to meet like-minded people who share your enthusiasm for the work and the man.

DO JOIN US

Contact: Diana Scotney the Membership Secretary on 01462-623941. e-mail dianascotney@virginmedia.com or go to www.terencerattigansociety.co.uk

Variation on a Theme

Terence Rattigan

SAMUELFRENCH.COM
SAMUELFRENCH-LONDON.CO.UK

FOR PRODUCTION ENQUIRIES

UNITED STATES AND CANADA
Info@SamuelFrench.com
1-866-598-8449

UNITED KINGDOM AND EUROPE
Plays@SamuelFrench-London.co.uk
020-7255-4302/01

Each title is subject to availability from Samuel French, depending
upon country of performance. Please be aware that *VARIATION ON
A THEME* may not be licensed by Samuel French in your territory.
Professional and amateur producers should contact the nearest Samuel
French office or licensing partner to verify availability.

VARIATION ON A THEME was first produced at the Globe Theatre, London, on May 8th, 1958. The performance was directed by John Gielgud and the cast was as follows:

ROSE.......................................Margaret Leighton
HETTIE......................................Jean Anderson
RON ....Jeremy Brett
KURT.......................................George Pravda
FIONA......................................Felicity Ross
MONA......................................Mavis Villiers
ADRIAN....................................Lawrence Dalzell
SAM ....Michael Goodliffe

ACT ONE

Scene One

(Scene: A terrace of a villa in the south of France.)

(What we see of the building shows its age, which is about eighty years, and its ancestry, which is grand-ducal. The terrace is broad and furnished with very comfortable-looking modern garden furniture.)

(The villa is in process of being done up for its present occupier; a tarpaulin covers some part of the outer wall, and the drawing-room, whose french windows give access to the terrace and into a part of which we may see, has its furniture covered in dust-sheets.)

(Steps left and right lead respectively to drive and front door, and garden and swimming-pool (both unseen).)

(It is just after sunrise. A woman of about sixty **(HETTIE)** *is snoozing, fully dressed, on a day bed with a blanket over her.* **ROSE** *comes up the steps left. She is in the middle thirties, beautiful and dressed (now in a dinner dress) with a style and elegance that has little to do with current fashion, and which one feels she has carefully studied to suit her personality.)*

(Not seeing **HETTIE** *she goes to a tray of drinks that is on a table backstage, and pours herself out a drink. At the sound of the soda water siphoning into the glass* **HETTIE** *wakes.)*

HETTIE. This is a hell of a time to come home.

ROSE. *(turning, startled)* Hettie – I told you not to wait up.

1

HETTIE. I know you did. I wasn't. My room was too damned hot and there was a blasted convocation of politic mosquitoes in there—

ROSE. There aren't any mosquitoes up here.

HETTIE. That's what *you* think. When you rename this place you should call it The Villa Moustique—

ROSE. *(angrily)* I hate you waiting up for me like this, Hettie. You do it every night I go out. It's not what I'm paying you for.

HETTIE. No. I suppose it isn't. What are you drinking?

ROSE. All right, all right. An orange squash and soda.

HETTIE. Let's see.

(She goes over to ROSE, *takes the drink from her hand and sniffs it suspiciously. Then she hands it back to her.)*

How many drinks did you have at the Casino?

ROSE. One.

HETTIE. Like hell—

ROSE. I had one brandy, and Lord knows I needed that. Let me tell you what happened—

(She suddenly looks contrite and with a quick movement kisses HETTIE *on the cheek.)*

I'm sorry, Hettie.

HETTIE. What about?

ROSE. That thing I just said about paying you.

HETTIE. Well, you do pay me, so why shouldn't you say so?

ROSE. Do you want me to answer that?

HETTIE. I'm a paid companion. Who cares? I don't. I'd only care if I were unpaid. Which I might be soon, the way things are going. How much did you lose down at the Casino tonight?

ROSE. Nothing. Well – four and a half thousand—

HETTIE. *(quickly)* Pounds?

ROSE. No, francs, for heaven's sake. When have I ever lost four and a half thousand pounds?

HETTIE. Not—let me see—since last Thursday.

ROSE. That was an exception. I just got carried away watching that fat man with all those big white plaques, and it wasn't four and a half. It was two. I'll get that back, don't worry. No, tonight was awful.

HETTIE. Four pounds ten awful?

ROSE. It was the way it happened. That's why I needed that brandy. *(Accusingly)* Hettie, do you realize you sent me out tonight without any money?

HETTIE. Oh God. did I? Sorry. Still, as you were with Kurt I thought—

ROSE. I ditched Kurt at Cannes—

HETTIE. Ditched fifty million?

ROSE. *(smiling)* Don't worry. Not for good. Only he bored me so much tonight, I could have screamed in his face. In fact I rather think I did. Well, anyway, I told him I had a migraine and as he wanted to go on trying to bust the Greek syndicate, I got clean away.

HETTIE. So you migrained Kurt? That was quite an achievement. So then?

ROSE. So then—as it was still quite early—

(**HETTIE** *looks at her watch.*)

(Impatiently) Listen, the doctor didn't say I had to be in bed by twelve every night of ray life—

HETTIE. *(quietly)* He did, you know.

ROSE. Well, anyway, it didn't seem late and I wanted a little more gambling so I stopped off at Juan. Well, there was practically no one there – only one table of chemmy left – but no seat and there was a bank that had gone a couple of times – a terrible woman with a squint was running it – so I walked up and said banco. I got an eight – and—

HETTIE. *(simultaneously, with* **ROSE***)* She had a nine.

ROSE. That's right. So I opened my bag with that bright smile I keep for losing bets – and well – nothing. Not one blasted franc.

HETTIE. But they must have known who you were.

ROSE. If they did they concealed it pretty well. Anyway, I haven't been to Juan for ages. There was the longest and iciest pause in world history while I fumbled away in my bag – with that smile becoming glassier every second – producing bric-à-brac—

HETTIE. Look, love, there's bric-à-brac and bric-à-brac. Surely that cigarette-case—

ROSE. Have some sense, Hettie. Did you want me to throw a cigarette-case on to the table and say: 'This is genuine Fabergé, given me by my second husband – the Marquis de Beaupré; oh, and by the way, these pearls were given me by my very last husband, Michael Bradford – that's the film star, and these emeralds by the gentleman I'm walking out with at the moment – Kurt Mast – you know – the financier'?

HETTIE. You didn't need to do any of that, but you could surely have told them who you were.

ROSE. And who am I? You tell me.

HETTIE. They'd have recognized the name.

ROSE. Which one?

HETTIE. The one you were born with, idiot. The one the papers call you by.

ROSE. Supposing they hadn't. Anyway, you know I loathe it. I don't know why the papers use it all the time. My right name is Bradford and will be until it is or isn't Mast. Anyway, I challenge anyone to face a woman with a squint that one owes four and a half thousand francs to and say, 'Madame, I happen to be—' *(She stops and turns to the drink tray.)* I'm going to have a drink.

(As HETTIE *looks at her)*

He only said 'not too much'. He didn't say 'nothing at all'.

HETTIE. I know. I heard him.

(Watching ROSE *pouring out a brandy)* Only I doubt
if he recommended brandy at five-thirty in the
morning.

ROSE. He doesn't know a damn thing – that silly little
doctor. I'm going to try another one.

HETTIE. Why not? You only need one more for game.

(After a pause) You don't even like saying it, do you?

ROSE. What?

HETTIE. Your name.

ROSE. I've told you. It isn't my name.

HETTIE. Well – so what *did* you do to this woman with the
squint?

ROSE. I faced her with a frank and honest gaze – only it was
a bit difficult not knowing which eye to try to be frank
and honest into – and said, I'm afraid, Madam, I've
come out without any money and shall have to give
you a cheque. Faultless French, a winning, apologetic
smile, sincere charm oozing – but no damn good.
Pandemonium. The usual little character with the
usual spade beard summoned out of the office and I'd
have been off to the clink, I suppose – if it hadn't been
for this young man—

HETTIE. Ah. Now we come to the point.

ROSE. Oh no. No point.

HETTIE. Sure?

ROSE. Quite sure.

HETTIE. Why?

ROSE, A pompadour to here. *(She indicates a lofty hair style.)*

HETTIE. Hell, these days that could mean he's the Olympic
welter-weight champion.

ROSE. This one's a ballet dancer.

HETTIE. So?

ROSE. So he's also got a friend. Nice and quiet, but very
firm, and very wary. The boy's hell, anyway, I may say.
The show-off of the world. Apparently he knew who

I was because I met him in Sophie – what's-her-name's dressing-room one evening. He was flattering about the white Balenciaga I was wearing that night. Have you got four five on you, Hettie?

HETTIE. No. I'll have to go upstairs to the safe. Why?

ROSE. Because they're coming up to collect it.

HETTIE. When? Tomorrow?

ROSE. No. Tonight. I mean this morning. They wanted to play another shoe. As soon as that's finished—

HETTIE. *(angrily)* Rose – for God's sake! Honestly, sometimes I think you really *are* round the bend—

ROSE. Well, I've got to pay them back, haven't I, and they live in Monte—

HETTIE. Is there a postal strike on?

ROSE. Well, they so obviously wanted to be asked. The boy anyway. He's heard about the new house—

HETTIE. *(looking at the shrouded sitting-room)* A lot you'll have to show him, won't you? Rose – honestly! You'll be kept up at least another hour – and just to impress a chorus boy with an unfinished, mosquito-ridden, draughty old villa—

ROSE. Ah. But built by the Grand Duke Auguste. And he's not a chorus boy. He dances Spectre de la Rose and the Blue Bird. And the friend's very grand indeed. A famous choreographer. He did the dances for that musical we saw in New York the night we sailed. *(Impatiently)* All right, Hettie, I'll sleep all day tomorrow.

HETTIE. You won't. You've got that lunch party.

ROSE. Oh yes. Well, in the afternoon—

HETTIE. Tea with Mona and cocktails with the Johnsons—

ROSE. Oh well. What the hell!

HETTIE. As you say. What the hell. I'll meet them, give them the money and a drink, and show them over the ruins. You go to bed.

ROSE. No point. I wouldn't sleep anyway.

HETTIE. Take something.

ROSE. I took two last night. I don't want to become a junkie like Mona—

HETTIE. What stops you sleeping? Is it— *(She puts her hand on her lung.)*

ROSE. Oh, no. I don't feel that at all these days.

HETTIE. Then what—?

ROSE. *(lightly)* God knows. Remorse, I suppose, for a life of guilt and shame. *(Seeing* **HETTIE**'s *eyes on her)* I just don't sleep well. Lots of people don't sleep well. *(She looks over the side of the terrace.)* Why does a sunrise on this coast always look like a cheap water-colour? Pale and mean and sort of fetid?

HETTIE. *(shrugging)* Because that's exactly what this coast is, I suppose.

ROSE. That's just fashionable talk, Hettie. This coast is all right. It's corny and vulgar, but it's fun – like Blackpool or Atlantic City. You mustn't take the people's pleasures away from us. *(She turns to listen.)* That's the car. They've found the house all right.

HETTIE. Not so hard considering you can practically see it from Marseilles.

ROSE. *(leaning over railings left and calling)* Hullo. I'm on the terrace. *(She turns to* **HETTIE**.*)* A pale blue Thunderbird.

HETTIE. You amaze me.

*(***RON*** comes on. He is about twenty-six, dressed in sports clothes, with an elaborate 'Tony Curtis' hair style.)*

ROSE. I'm glad you made it. Where's your friend?

RON. He went back to Monte. He asked me to make his apologies, but he was feeling most tired.

(He speaks with a very indeterminate accent, vaguely French, vaguely Russian and basically English Midlands.)

ROSE. But I thought you came over to Juan together. How did he get back?

RON. Oh – taxi.

ROSE. *(rather wickedly)* Then that beautiful blue object down there is yours, is it?

RON. No. Not really. But he is a rich choreographer and can afford a taxi, and I am only a poor dancer and cannot.

ROSE. Oh, I see. *(Preparing to introduce* **HETTIE***)* By the way, I'm absolutely terrible about names, and yours *is* rather difficult.

RON. Anton Valov.

ROSE. Oh yes, of course. Monsieur Valov – Lady Henrietta Crichton-Parry,

HETTIE. ⎫
⎬ *(murmuring)* How do you do?
RON. ⎭

HETTIE. Can I get you a drink?

RON. *(who has plainly been impressed by the title)* Oh, but Lady Henrietta – can't I—

HETTIE. No. Getting drinks is part of my duties. The pleasantest part. What's it to be?

RON. Have you any vin rosé?

HETTIE. Of course.

RON. *(to* **ROSE***)* This is a magnificent view. The best I have ever seen, I think – except possibly for Mabel Penrhyn's at Gap Ferrat.

ROSE. Who's Mabel Penrhyn?

RON. The Countess of Penrhyn. You do not know her? That surprises me. Everybody knows her.

ROSE. Ah, but then, you see, I don't know everybody. And she has a good view?

RON. Magnificent. But of course I am seeing this at dawn which is a great privilege. I think dawn in the south of France surpasses any sight of the kind anywhere else in the world. *(With a wide gesture)* The colour. It is magnificent, is it not? Oh. Excuse me.

(HETTIE has approached with his uin rosé and his expansive gesture has nearly knocked it out of her hand.)

HETTIE. That's quite all right.

RON. Yes. The mystery and magic of the Riviera dawn never fails – does it?

(HETTIE and ROSE have exchanged a glance.)

ROSE. *(at length)* No. *(She turns to HETTIE.)* Hettie, dear, would you get Monsieur Valov the money I owe him?

RON. *(with a gesture of apparent embarrassment)* Oh no – please.

ROSE. *(showing her irritation)* You don't want it back?

RON. At your convenience.

ROSE. This is my convenience. *(To HETTIE)* And get me a brandy and soda on the way – would you, dear?

HETTIE. *(as she goes)* No. You can damn well dig your own grave.

(She goes out into the sitting-room. ROSE smiles, looks at the drink tray, decides against it and sits down.)

RON. *(trying to keep the awe out of his voice)* Lady Henrietta Crichton-Parry – she must be a daughter of the Duke of Ayrshire, is she not?

ROSE. Yes. That's right.

RON. And she has been working for you long?

ROSE. Two years.

RON. *Tiens. C'est amusant, ca!*

ROSE. *Qu'est ce qui est amusant?*

RON. *(switching quickly. His accent was not as good as hers.)* A duke's daughter working as a housekeeper—

ROSE. Social secretary.

RON. Well – whatever it is called – I thought the family was well off.

ROSE. *(her voice gradually acquiring an edge to it)* I suppose they were once. So was she. Unhappily they had death duties and she had an infallible system at roulette. She

needed a job quickly and was lucky to get this one.
I was lucky to get her. I think that exhausts the subject,
don't you?

(Pause)

RON. *(playfully)* Dear Madame la Marquise de Beaupré is
a little angry with me, I think. She must not be. She
must remember that a humble ballet dancer must
always be curious about the ways and manners of the
great world.

(There is another pause.)

ROSE. *(at length)* Look, Monsieur Valov – just three points.
First, I'm not angry with you at all. Only perhaps a little
tired and I'm sorry if I showed it just now. Secondly,
regarding Madame la Marquise de Beaupré. I'm afraid
you're two whole husbands out.

RON. Oh, my God! Mrs. Michael Bradford. Of course. I am
so sorry.

ROSE. That's all right. It's hard to keep pace, I know. Now
the last point. You may be a bit offended by this,
but please, please try not to be. All my life I've been
irritated to death by phoney accents. Now, would you
mind really dreadfully if you dropped that one of
yours and reverted to your native Birmingham?

(Pause)

RON. I beg your pardon.

ROSE. It *is* Birmingham, isn't it? I'm very rarely wrong.

RON. *(stiffly, still with accent)* I am afraid I do not
understand—

ROSE. You see, I spent the first twenty years of my life in
Frogmore Road, off Five Towns Avenue, and I can spot
a Brum accent a mile away. I expect you can with me
too. We never really lose it, do we? I'd guess you come
from somewhere much more posh than Frogmore
Road. Say the North Side. Am I right?

(**RON** *stares at her, still acting polite bewilderment.*
HETTIE *comes in with some notes in her hand.*)

What have you been doing? Reading my old love
letters?

HETTIE. That's a show-off – pretending to your guest that
the people who loved you could actually write. No.
There are more interesting things in that safe than
love letters.

ROSE. Such as?

HETTIE. Accounts.

ROSE. *(yawning)* Oh. Those.

HETTIE. *(to Ron)* It *was* four thousand five, wasn't it?

RON. *(still with accent)* No. Four thousand, three fifty. See,
I will give you change.

(**HETTIE** *glances at him. He does not meet her gaze. She
shrugs sadly.* **RON** *gives* **HETTIE** *some coins and takes
the notes from her.*)

HETTIE. An honest man – on this coast! Fancy. Well, I'm
to bed. *(To* **RON***)* Please don't keep her up too long,
Monsieur Valov. You have an invalid on your hands.

RON. *(still with accent)* Oh, I am most sorry to hear that.
What is the trouble?

HETTIE. Consumption.

ROSE. *(angrily)* Oh really, Hettie – you live in a Victorian
dream world. *(To* **RON***)* I have a slight lung condition,
Monsieur Valov, which is in process of being cured by
an antibiotic called streptomycin—

HETTIE. Which makes her pass out every time they give it
her—

ROSE. A little allergy, which is perfectly natural. They're
giving me a lovely new pill now—

HETTIE. Which she washes down with gulps of brandy she's
been strictly forbidden even to sniff.

ROSE. Oh, go to bed, Hettie. I'm quite sure you're boring
Monsieur Valov as much as you're boring me.

HETTIE. Well, good night. Good *dawn*, I mean.

(She goes out. There is a pause. ROSE *goes to the drink
tray.)*

ROSE. Let me replenish.

(RON *walks slowly over to her with his empty glass. She
takes the bottle which* **HETTIE** *has opened and fills his
glass. Then she pours out a brandy and soda for herself.)*

RON. *(pointing to her glass)* 'Ere – you didn't oughter-'ve
done that, did yer, girl?

ROSE. *(answering in similar Birmingham accent.)* You're
bloomin' right – I didn't oughter – but I done it, see.

(She laughs softly – pleased with him for the first time.)

(Touching his sleeve and reverting to her normal accent)
Thank you and sorry. But mostly thank you.

RON. You got the district wrong. Acacia Avenue.

ROSE. Off Leamington Road? Oh, that's real posh. Did you
ever go to the Warwick Arms?

RON. You bet I did. I didn't drink then, mind you. I was
training for the ballet. But I used to pop in there quite
often on Saturday nights.

*(He now speaks with his natural voice which still has a
trace of the Midlands.)*

ROSE. That's when they had 'Harry's Hotspurs' playing in
the lounge. Oh no – of course that'd be before your
time.

RON. No, they were still there in fifty-two. Bloody awful
they were, too.

ROSE. Were they? I used to think they were wonderful. In
fact my idea of heaven was to get someone to take me
there Saturday night, give me a 'gin and It' and let me
listen to *It's a Lovely Day Tomorrow*, by special request of
Miss Rose Fish.

RON. When did you leave Brum?

ROSE. The year the war ended.

RON. *(admiringly)* You've come quite a way in that time, haven't you?

ROSE. Quite a way. So have you.

RON. Oh, *I* haven't started. I haven't got anywhere yet. But I will, you know. All those geezers that read palms and crystals and things – they all say I've got it.

ROSE. What? Talent?

RON. No. Money. It's the same thing, isn't it?

ROSE. Yes. I suppose so. *(The topic seems to bore her. She turns brusquely to the gramophone.)* What sort of music do you like, Mr— what *is* your real name?

RON. Vale. Ron Vale.

ROSE. But why did you change it? It's a good name. Surely this Anton Valov stuff is dated now, isn't it?

RON. Not in France. They're old-fashioned here. Anywhere else in the world Ronald Vale would be great. But here – oh yes, they've heard of the Royal Ballet all right, and they think Fonteyn and Soames and Ashton are fine, but to them ballet still really means Diaghilev and Fokine and Karsavina and the full Russian chi-chi. Besides, it pays down here to have a bit of mystery about one's nationality—

ROSE. Pays? In what way?

RON. Oh, a lot of ways. *You'd* be surprised.

ROSE. I don't think I would. What music?

RON. *(coming to the gramophone)* Oh, anything. Not ballet.

ROSE. Rock 'n' roll? Classical? Something romantic?

RON. Something romantic.

(Suddenly, and with great assurance, he throws his arms around her and tries to kiss her. Quite gently, but with expertise matching his assurance, she pushes him away.)

ROSE. We'll have what's on.

(She switches on the machine. After a moment we hear the overture to 'Traviata'.)

Damn. That's not my choice. It must be Fiona's.

RON. Fiona?

ROSE. My daughter. She's sixteen, and like you, she has a taste for romantic music. I'm afraid I haven't.

(She switches the gramophone off. She is looking among records when RON *walks brusquely up to her and turns her round to face him.)*

RON. I know just what you're thinking.

ROSE. Do you?

RON. You're thinking – this one isn't on the level. You're thinking of Sam—

ROSE. Sam?

RON. Sam Duveen. The choreographer. *(As she still looks blank)* The chap I was at the Casino with.

ROSE. *(quietly)* Oh. Well, do you know, Mr Vale, I wasn't thinking of Sam Duveen. I really wasn't. Now what record shall we have?

RON. *(turning her round again)* Oh yes, I know. That's the impression I give. It's not my fault. All right – I could wear my hair differently, but why should I?

ROSE. Why indeed?

RON. It's being in the ballet too. You girls never give us the benefit of the doubt, do you? *(Fiercely)* Sam Duveen's just a good friend of mine and that's that—

ROSE. You really mustn't disturb yourself like this, Mr. Vale. All I know, or indeed care, about your friend Sam Duveen is that he did some very good dances for a musical I once saw and that he has a very nice pale blue Thunderbird. Now please help me choose.

RON. *(darkly)* There's a crack in that, too – I know. All right – so he lets me drive his car. All right, so I live in his villa at Monte. All right, if you like, so for all I know he maybe— but that doesn't make *me,* does it?

(**ROSE**, *failing advice from* **RON**, *has finally chosen a record and put it on.*)

ROSE. This is harmless. It's called 'Background Music for Talking'. Go on, please.

(She sits down far away from him. He follows her.)

RON. I can't help what he feels about me, can I?

ROSE. *(quietly)* Since you ask me, Mr. Vale, I have to answer that I should think you probably can. Now let's talk about something else.

RON. Do you believe what I've just been saying?

ROSE. I'm not very clear about what you've just been saying.

RON. Do you believe I go for women?

ROSE. *(after a pause)* I believe it quite probable that you go for those women who go for you.

RON. *(desperately)* Well – do you believe I go for you?

ROSE. In view of my last answer, I can't quite see that the question applies.

RON. *(smiling appreciatively)* God, you're good. You're not just good, you're great. I'm beginning to see—

(There is the sound of a car.)

ROSE. Oh damn!

RON. Who'd come visiting at this time?

ROSE. *(urgently)* Turn that light out.

RON. *(struggling with a table lamp)* Where's the switch?

KURT. *(off, calling)* Rose? You up?

ROSE. It's too late. *(Calling, wearily)* Come on up. Kurt.

RON. *(looking over railings)* God. What a car! And a chauffeur. At six in the morning, yet!

ROSE. *(shrugging)* He's got six chauffeurs yet.

RON. This is Kurt Mast, isn't it?

(**ROSE** *nods.*)

Wow! This is the life all right—

(**KURT MAST** *appears on the terrace. He is in the late thirties, and rather handsome in an unsmiling, uncharming way. His clothes (lounge suit now) are made in London and he speaks English well without a strong accent, but his English vocabulary and phrasing, learnt mainly by contact with American occupation troops after the war, is sometimes incongruously inelegant.*)

(*Taking no notice of* **RON** *he walks straight up to* **ROSE** *and kisses her.*)

KURT. Migraine better?

ROSE. Not really. (*Pointing to* **RON**) This is—

(**KURT**, *without looking at* **RON**, *goes to the gramophone and turns it off. Then he goes back to* **ROSE**.)

KURT. You should be hitting the hay with the aspirin and the supponeryls. It's damn fool stuff sitting up like this.

ROSE. I suppose so. May I introduce—

KURT. I was on my way up to the villa and from the road I see the light on this terrace, and I see you moving about so I said, Jeez, this dame, when will she learn some sense? I'll *go* in and tell her where she is getting off. So now I am telling you. It was two thirty-five when you left me. What in hell are you doing for three and a half hours?

ROSE. For some of the time I have been talking to Mr Anton Valov here. Mr Valov – Mr Mast.

(*At last* **KURT** *turns and glances at* **RON**, *who smiles warmly at him.* **KURT** *does not return the smile, but nods in greeting.*)

KURT. How do you do?

(*They shake hands.*)

You are Russian?

RON. No. English.

KURT. (*approvingly*) Fine. fine. (*He turns abruptly back to* **ROSE**.) Baby, oh baby, did I carve up that Greek syndicate tonight. I am telling you I carved them in slices, *(He makes the appropriate gesture.)* We will eat them tomorrow night with a thick mushroom sauce at the Chateau de Madrid. *(Holding her hands)* We must be there at a quarter to nine.

ROSE. It rather depends how I feel.

KURT. *(with a glint of steel)* You will feel well tomorrow. No migraine tomorrow. So I will call for you at seven-thirty and be punctual, please. Her Highness must not be kept waiting.

ROSE. Lottie? She's been kept waiting all her life. For a free meal she'd wait until the Mediterranean froze over.

KURT. *(after a pause)* Tomorrow night I am not keeping the princess waiting.

ROSE. Quite right. You mustn't ever lose your reputation for exquisite manners.

KURT. *(after another pause)* Your migraine must be good and bad tonight, I think. You said things, too, at the Casino, I am remembering. *(With a jovial laugh)* It's no good, baby. If ever you want Kurt out of your life, you'll need more than wisecracks. But you don't want Kurt out of your life, do you, my baby? And you won't ever, will you?

(He puts his arms around her.)

ROSE. Something tells me that just at the moment we're not being awfully entertaining to Mr Valov. *(She breaks free and turns to* **RON***.)* Can I get you another drink?

RON. No, thank you. *(Diffidently)* I was thinking that perhaps I'd better—

ROSE. *(firmly)* Certainly not. I won't hear of your going. You must forgive Kurt's vocabulary, Mr Valov. He learnt his English in the American Zone. Most Americans, I know, speak far better English than we do, but Kurt doesn't seem to have met them, which, as he was very actively engaged in the black market at the time, is hardly surprising. Now, please let me get you just one more glass of rosé.

RON. Thank you.

(She takes his glass and goes to the drink tray.)

ROSE. Kurt?

KURT. Are you crazy?

ROSE. I thought perhaps a coca-cola.

KURT. No, thank you.

(He is staring at **RON**, *taking him in for the first time. He seems puzzled.)*

KURT. It is late, isn't it, Mr. Valov, for you to be out visiting?

ROSE. *(from the drink tray)* Mr. Valov could easily say the same of you, couldn't he? Here, Mr. Valov.

(She hands **RON** *his drink,* **KURT** *looks from one to the other, then enlightenment suddenly dawns.)*

KURT. I got it. He's a journalist.

ROSE. *(quickly silencing* **RON**.*)* How did you guess so quickly?

KURT. They are not fooling me. Nowadays they dress so as not to look like journalists, but I can always spot them. You are interviewing Miss Fish?

RON. Well—

ROSE. Yes – he's interviewing me.

KURT. It is smart to catch her at this hour. You would not be catching her in the day. What paper?

ROSE. The *Daily Mail.*

KURT. An excellent paper. You will please to say nothing about the American Zone and the black market, remembering please that Miss Fish likes her little funny jokes, but you may say you met me, and that the wedding is to be on December 17th in Düsseldorf – which is my birthday—

RON. *(entering more into the spirit)* Is it indeed? I see. Thank you.

KURT. You will also want to know why I am quarrelling with the *Daily Express* and Mr Sefton Delmer. I will tell you. I am not making fusses about the expression 'Gutter

Tycoon' or his joke about 'Back street boy makes bad', because I am not ashamed I come from the working class, and I am not objecting to the story that I was buying war junk from the Americans in forty-five and selling it back to them in the Korean War at ten times the money. So is only good business. No, sir. Financiers are always goddam villains and so are Germans always goddam villains, and German financiers are the goddamdest villains in the world, especially one who is beginning in a cellar in Düsseldorf with fifty occupation pfennigs in his pocket and is ending in the Schloss Guldheim with fifty million West German marks – so I am not caring a tinker's nickel what the press is saying about me. But 'neo-Nazi'—now that I am not taking. Jeez, I am not taking that. You can quote this. Kurt Mast is a social democrat.

ROSE. Is that the way you voted in the last election, Kurt?

KURT. In the last election I was not voting at all. I wasn't even voting for Adenauer. By God, I wasn't. By sincere conviction am I a social democrat. *(To* RON*)* You got that straight, bud?

RON. Yes. Quite straight.

KURT. Neo-Nazi! Where are they getting such stuff from? That's criminal talk. O.K. So that's all, I guess. Any questions?

RON. No, I don't think so.

KURT. You're a smart kid. Working at six in the morning. That's the way I made it – maybe that's the way you'll make it. O.K. I am not interrupting you and Miss Fish any more. *(He turns to* ROSE.*)* Goodnight, baby,

(He tries to kiss her on the lips, but she offers her cheek, which he is forced to accept.)

KURT. Sleep well. Take those pills. They're good – non-toxic – the latest. I had them flown over specially. *(He pats her familiarly on the behind.)* No migraine tomorrow. Seven-thirty sharp, if you please.

(He turns abruptly and goes out. There is a pause.)

ROSE. *(at length)* I'm sorry.

RON. I enjoyed it.

ROSE. He's scared of journalists. I knew it would get rid of him pretty quick.

RON. Is that the way to talk about the man you're going to marry?

ROSE. It's the way to talk about Kurt Mast.

RON. You'll get a good settlement, I hope.

ROSE. Are you kidding? I'm settling for half the Ruhr.

(**RON** *laughs and raises his glass.*)

RON. Well – congratulations.

ROSE. I think you really mean that.

(Pause)

RON. Well, if you don't like this tycoon, why not get yourself another?

ROSE. When you get to know tycoons as well as I do, which one day I'm quite sure you will – *(mischievously)* female ones, I mean for you, of course – you'll find that they don't usually come complete with good figures and handsome faces. Kurt is a pretty rare specimen.

(**RON** *gets up and walks gracefully past* **ROSE***, the object of the journey being to replace his glass on the tray, and of the exercise, to impress* **ROSE** *with his figure.*)

RON. My God – do you think *that's* a good figure?

ROSE. *(watching him, amused)* Only by tycoon standards. Not by ballet, of course. Pour yourself another rosé.

RON. No. I mustn't disobey instructions and keep you up. Before I go though, do tell me one thing. How did all this start?

ROSE. All what?

RON. You know. This. *(He waves his hand to indicate the villa.)* Lords, Marquises, film stars and tycoons. Who was the very first?

(There is a pause while **ROSE** *coolly measures the degree of his impertinence. Then she decides to answer him.)*

ROSE. A solicitor called Peter Hawkins – of Gartwright and Hawkins, twenty-three Commerce Square, and he lived in Edgbaston. In 1943 he was my boss and I married him. He died two years later and left me a little money. With that I came down here and met – people—

RON. You say he was your boss? But you were on the stage, weren't you?

ROSE. I certainly wasn't. Where did that story start? I was a respectable girl I'll have you know. I was a typist.

RON. *(laughing)* You were what?

ROSE. What's the joke?

RON. *(still laughing)* You – a typist! I'm just picturing it – you bent over a typewriter, with the bracelets jangling and the pearls getting all caught up in the machinery—

ROSE. *(acidly)* I didn't have pearls or bracelets then, you know.

RON. Listen, I'll swallow most things. Old gullible Ron – they call me. But this is too much. You, a typist! But that, no!

*(***ROSE,*** after an angry glance at him, disappears quickly into the sitting-room, emerging in a second with a portable typewriter and a sheet of typing paper. She sets the typewriter up on a table, opens it up and with plainly practised dexterity inserts the sheet of paper. Then she sits down – her back towards us – savagely pulls off her bracelets, and flexes her fingers.)*

ROSE. All right. Now dictate something.

RON. Dictate? What?

ROSE. *(speaking very deliberately)* Dictate anything you like, but at roughly this speed. You don't need to go slower. All right. Go ahead.

(Pause)

RON. Dear Mrs Bradford, dear Marquise de Beaupré, dear Lady – hell, what was it? – Huntercombe – dear Mrs. Hawkins – and I've quite likely left out one – dear Miss Fish – anyway – this is a message for you from Ron Vale.

(**ROSE**, *appearing to take no notice of the words, types with quiet, evidently highly practised and methodical speed. As he pauses for inspiration she stops and looks down at the typewriter.*)

Ever since I came into Sophie's dressing-room that night and saw you standing there in that white dress I have not been able to think of anything else. You are just about the most beautiful thing I ever saw in all my born—

ROSE. *(quietly)* Too fast.

RON. The most beautiful thing I ever saw in all my born days – and to meet you tonight, and talk to you, and be asked up to this house has been just about the greatest thrill of my life.

(He stops for a moment.)

I want to say I am sorry I tried my phoney accent on you, but that was only because I was shy, and wanted to impress – as per usual, I am afraid.

(He stops again.)

Thank you for letting me come up here tonight and I would like to point out while I have the chance that it is a hell of a way from here to Monte Carlo – especially driving at this time in the morning after a few drinks. That is all, I think – except I still do not bloody well believe you were ever a typist.

(He has gone faster at the end, and it is a few seconds before **ROSE** *completes her methodical typing. Then she pulls out the sheet from the machine, turns and hands it to him. He stares at her for a moment, searching in her face for an answer to his unspoken question, but she turns and lights a cigarette.)*

ROSE. Correct?

RON. *(glancing at the page) A* hundred per. All right. I take it back. You *were* a typist.

ROSE. And a very good one, too.

(She comes and takes the page out of his hand, reading it. He looks down at the top of her head, uncertain and puzzled.)

RON. *(at length)* Well?

ROSE. *(not looking up)* Well what?

RON. *(brusquely, daring all)* Well, am I staying or going?

(Pause, **ROSE** *still is scrutinizing the paper.)*

ROSE. I did make a mistake. I spelt 'born' wrong—

*(***RON*** *angrily snatches the paper from her hand.)*

RON. I'm keeping this as a souvenir. I hope you don't mind. *(He folds the paper and puts it in his pocket.)* Good night and thank you for your hospitality.

(He bows with rather ludicrous formality and goes towards the steps.)

ROSE. Mr. Vale—

(He stops and turns.)

RON. My name is Ron.

ROSE. Please don't be angry with me, Ron. I'd hate that because I'm really very grateful to you for the compliment you've just paid me. Please say you're not angry.

RON. *(shortly)* That's all right. I quite realize I'm not Kurt Mast. I quite realize I haven't got anything to offer—

ROSE. *(sincerely)* But really you have a lot to offer. An awful lot. I know there are many, many women in the world who must find you devastatingly attractive—

RON. But you're not one of them, eh?

ROSE. Well, you see, I've never in all my life found any man devastatingly attractive. Just as well, or I might have been devastated, and that would never have done – dear Ron, you do see that I'm not really an awfully nice or rewarding person and in a few minutes, when you're bowling along the Monte Carlo road in your pretty blue Thunderbird, congratulate yourself on being well out of what would have been an utterly pointless little adventure. Goodnight.

(She goes to him and shakes his hand.)

Incidentally, next time you're this way, please do come up – have a drink and meet some of my friends—

(**RON**, *angrily, pushes her away from him.*)

RON. You think that's all I'm after, don't you – to get where I can come up here when I like, have a drink and meet your smart, rich friends? That's what you think, isn't it?

(**ROSE**, *looking at him with some sympathy and understanding, does not reply.*)

RON. *(roughly)* Isn't it?

ROSE. That one I don't answer, Ron.

RON, *(violently)* Well, it isn't bloody true, see. Do you know what I'm after? Just one thing. I'm after you.

(**ROSE** *continues to look at him. He angrily stubs out a cigarette.*)

Well, I'm off.

ROSE. *(quietly)* How old are you, Ron?

RON. *(turning)* Twenty-six.

(**ROSE** *nods.*)

Listen – put *that* thought right out of your head. I've never gone for the young ones anyway. I prefer older women, and I always say that when two people have a real *rapport* the question of disparity of age just doesn't arise—

(**ROSE** *throws her head back and laughs with real enjoyment.*)

(Bewildered) What's the joke?

ROSE. Just that it might have been myself talking to my second husband in our walking-out days. I used that word *rapport* too. Only my prospective victim was in the late fifties, and as of now, I can still put money on my own age on a roulette table. Only just, I grant, but then you're in the dernière douzaine, too. No, Ron, I don't think it's age that's the problem between us—

(RON, prepared for one last try, walks towards her and takes her hand.)

RON. *(tenderly)* What is it that's the problem between us?

(Pause)

ROSE. *(with sudden and genuine misery)* Oh, I don't know, Just me, I suppose. Just me and what I am.

RON. Forget it.

ROSE. *You* be me and try to forget it!

(A thought strikes her and she laughs.)

Come to think of it you *are* me. At least – me nine years younger. That's funny – you being me – that's awfully funny. Ron minus Acacia Avenue equals Rose minus Frogmore Road. So cancel out Birmingham on either side and what have you got? You've got Ron equals Rose. Rose equals Ron. If you really do like me at all you're a narcissist, Ron.

RON. *(his face close to hers)* I'm not listening. I'm just looking. Christ – you're beautiful. Given half a chance I could go for you the way I've never gone for anyone before.

(He draws her towards him. This time she does not try to evade him, nor resists when he kisses her. Eventually she disengages herself gently and pats his cheek.)

ROSE. You'd better put your car in the garage. Otherwise there'll be too much speculation among the servants. Some we can hardly avoid—

(He kisses her on the forehead with a brief, triumphant smile. Then he turns quickly and walks to the steps, goes

*down them and disappears towards the drive. We hear
the car's engine being started up.)*

*(ROSE, meanwhile, has looked after him, her expression
troubled. Then she wanders to the drink tray. She is
pouring herself out a brandy and soda as FIONA, her
daughter, appears suddenly in the french windows. She
is in a bathing-dress, and carries a towel and a portable
record-player. She stops at the sight of her mother, then
walks towards the steps right. ROSE sees her.)*

Fiona. You're up very early.

FIONA. No, not really. I always have a bathe before breakfast
and I have my breakfast at seven.

ROSE. Is that so? I didn't know.

FIONA. I don't want to waste the sun, you see.

ROSE. Yes. You're quite right. *(She kisses her on the cheek.)*
Good morning.

FIONA. Good morning, Mummy.

ROSE. What did you do last night?

FIONA. Oh, I had dinner up here with Hettie, and then
I went down to the Ciel et Enfer.

ROSE. Ciel et Enfer? What's that? A night club?

FIONA. No. It's just a café. Upstairs is just ordinary – that's
Ciel. Downstairs is much more fun. That's Enfer – and
it's where all the interesting people go. Jean-Louis
took me down on his Vespa.

ROSE. Jean-Louis? That's the boy who's writing the novel?

FIONA. Yes. Hettie made a terrible boob. She went and
asked him if it was existentialist.

ROSE. What was so wrong about that?

FIONA. *(genuinely shocked)* Mummy – existentialism's had it
years ago.

ROSE. Has it? I didn't know,

FIONA. It's as old-fashioned as Angry Young Men, or James
Deanery.

ROSE. Is it really? What's his novel about then?

FIONA. Oh, about a lot of young people who have love affairs with each other and don't much enjoy it, but go on doing it because there isn't any point in doing anything else.

ROSE. It sounds fascinating.

FIONA. Oh, it is. It's an advance on straightforward 'Je m'en foutisme' you see. The two main characters actually fall in love – I mean, real nineteenth-century love – not being able to do without each other and all that – and die together in a suicide pact.

ROSE. That sounds very romantic.

FIONA. That's his school – neo-romantic. It's the very latest St. Germain. Well—

*(She moves towards the steps right. **ROSE** looks at her.)*

ROSE. Are you doing anything tomorrow night, Fiona?

FIONA. *(a shade suspiciously)* No, Mummy. Why?

ROSE. *(nervously)* I wondered if you'd like, perhaps, to have an evening with me. Just the two of us.

FIONA. *(after a pause, without enthusiasm)* Yes, Mummy. That'd be fun.

ROSE. I've seen so little of you since you arrived. We could go and have dinner somewhere up in the mountains, perhaps, and afterwards you could take me to this Ciel et Enfer.

FIONA. *(after a pause)* You wouldn't like it at all.

ROSE, How do you know I wouldn't?

FIONA. I just know, that's all. It's not for you, Mummy. Not Enfer, anyway.

ROSE. You mean everyone there is very young?

FIONA. No. There are some quite old people there. There's a painter and his wife there every night and they're both well over forty. It's just – well— *(She pauses.)* Anyway, you'd be dressed all wrong.

ROSE. I could wear slacks-and do my hair in a fringe—

(FIONA *smiles – not rudely – but conclusively.* ROSE *turns away from her abruptly.*)

Don't use the springboard. It needs repairing.

FIONA. No, Mummy.

(She goes out. ROSE *goes to the railings to watch her.* RON *comes slowly up on to the terrace, sees* ROSE'*s back but does not go immediately to her, as his supposed ardour might seem to demand. Instead he looks up at the façade of the house, and then down at the view. Finally he joins* ROSE *at the railings, and slips an arm possessively around her waist.)*

RON. Your daughter?

*(*ROSE *nods.)*

Is she with you all the time?

ROSE. She was at boarding school in England until a month ago. Her choice. I don't go to England much. But I see as much of her as I can.

RON. Was her father the solicitor?

*(*ROSE *nods.)*

Skinny little mite. She doesn't look a bit like you.

ROSE. *(simply)* I don't know about that. I only know I love the way she looks. *(Calling, suddenly)* I said not the springboard, Fiona.

*(*RON *ducks quickly out of sight.)*

FIONA. *(calling, off)* It's all right, Mummy. I was only trying it.

RON. Did she see me?

ROSE. *(listlessly)* Maybe. I don't know. It doesn't matter anyway.

RON. She wouldn't think anything of it?

ROSE. Oh yes. Something. But not very much.

RON. You mean – she wouldn't be shocked?

ROSE. *(with a hard laugh)* That's straight from Acacia Avenue
– that question. *(She turns from gazing at her daughter
and looks at* RON.*)* No, she wouldn't be shocked. If
anything she'd be pleased. At least I'd be living up
to my reputation, which is just about the only thing
she enjoys about me. No, I'm afraid I don't shock my
daughter, Ron. I just bore her. I bore her to death.

RON. *(uncomfortably)* Do you mind?

ROSE. Yes.

*(She turns back to the railings and gazes down at the
swimming-pool.)*

RON. Have you got any others?

ROSE. No. She's the lot. *(With a smile)* I ought to have done
better with four husbands – oughtn't I? – but things
went a bit wrong after her.

RON. See much of her?

ROSE. As much as I can. The main reason I got this house
was because she adores the sun. *(Calling)* That's
enough, darling. Don't tire yourself out.

FIONA. *(off)* All right – Mummy.

(ROSE turns from watching FIONA.)

ROSE. *(at length)* Well, do you want me to show you your
room?

RON. Yes, please.

*(ROSE nods and goes slowly towards the sitting-room,
RON following. He stops at a vase.)*

Red roses. *(Pointing to another vase)* Red roses. *(At
another)* Red roses. I guess you like red roses.

ROSE. Red's my lucky colour, and Rose is my name. It's a
kind of superstition.

*(She takes both his hands, lowers her head and speaks
quickly and very quietly.)*

Listen, Monte Carlo isn't so far. I honestly do think
– for both our sakes—

RON. *(roughly)* Why are you so scared?

(He takes her by the shoulders and pushes her back to look into her eyes.)

ROSE. Me, scared? Really, Ron – you go too far.

RON. But you are, you know. Why?

(The strains of the overture to 'Trauiata' can be heard coming from the swimming-pool. ROSE goes quickly to the railings.)

(Calling) Not so loud, Fiona. You'll wake everyone up.

FIONA. *(off)* All right, Mummy.

(The record continues more softly.)

RON. Why are you scared?

(ROSE turns and looks at him.)

ROSE. I rather wish I knew.

(She goes to a vase, takes out a rose and puts it in his buttonhole. Then she kisses him lightly, takes a step back and looks at him.)

RON. *(holding her hand)* Well – shall we go?

(There is a pause. ROSE looks at him, then smiles.)

ROSE. *(at length, lightly)* Why not?

(Holding his hand she leads the way towards the french windows of the sitting-room. FIONA has turned up the volume of her record-player, and the strains of 'Traviata' are now again quite loud.)

(Curtain)

Scene Two

(Scene: The same, two months later.)

(The time is about eleven at night. The lights are on in the sitting-room, from which the dust sheets have now been removed, and a canasta four is in session there. The table is out of sight, but the players can occasionally be seen at the window as they move about.)

(On the terrace are **FIONA** *and* **HETTIE**. **FIONA** *is listening to a recording machine, prominently placed.* **HETTIE** *is knitting.)*

FIONA'S VOICE. *(from the machine)* – and so – all around us – ruin, shame, lies. So I dreamt, at moments, of meeting a man noble enough not to demand a mere reckoning of me, but to love me – Marguerite Gautier – to love the woman that I really am. This man might have been the Duke; but he is old, and old age cannot console me for the hell my life has fallen into. My heart has a need – a need that an older man cannot satisfy. Then – dear Armand – I met you – young, ardent, happy. In a minute – like some mad creature, I built a whole future on your love. I dreamt of the country, of purity, and I remembered my childhood – for whatever I may now have become, there was a time when, once, I was a child. Ah, but I was dreaming of what cannot be. Now – dear Armand – you know everything.

*(***FIONA*** switches it off.)*

FIONA. That's terrible, isn't it?

HETTIE. I'm prejudiced. I heard Bernhardt.

FIONA. You couldn't have.

HETTIE. Why the hell not? I was seven and she was a hundred and eight and it was in French and I didn't understand a damn word, but I still heard Bernhardt. You should do Juliet, dear – not this. Juliet's your age group.

FIONA. Yes, and she's the age group of every other girl trying to get into R.A.D.A. this year. Gosh, the number of potion scenes that must be spouted at those poor examiners every year! Makes one almost sorry for them. No, this is my lady.

HETTIE. Why?

FIONA. I don't know. I suppose because she's sold her soul to the devil.

HETTIE. Does that specially commend a part? Are we going to see you playing Faust some time?

FIONA. Oh, I don't love her only because she's wicked, but because she's honest and warm and brave and true and – oh, I don't know. I just love her, and I feel for her like mad, and I'm going to convey that feeling to the examiners even if I have to work on that machine all summer. I ought really to try and meet someone like that, I suppose, and study them at close quarters – but of course they don't exist nowadays.

HETTIE. Don't they?

FIONA. You mean Mona, or that Italian countess in there? Or that strip-tease girl Mummy brought up the other afternoon?

(HETTIE *says nothing.*)

Oh no, Hettie. They're just awful and sad and dull. I mean, there's no point in selling your soul to the devil these days – because the devil's got nothing to give you in return anyway. Of course in *her* day *(she points to the machine)* it was different. In yours too, I expect.

HETTIE. Possibly. I don't know. You see, I made no deal with Lucifer. In fact he never even made me an offer.

FIONA. But I bet it was fun, though, wasn't it – for the girls who did? Homburg and Aix-les-Bains, and enormous places in Scotland with sixty servants, and Vienna with the waltzes and special trains to Moscow to stay with a grand duke and – well – even this place. *(She looks up at the façade with distaste.)* Yes, even this place would have had a point then, I suppose.

HETTIE. Hasn't it now?

FIONA. No, of course it hasn't. Just a lot of unused bedrooms. What does luxury mean, Hettie? Only being able to live a life that no one else can afford. Look at Mona. With all her millions, does she ever take a special train anywhere? No. She goes on a tourist flight because there usually isn't a first class, and gets lunch trays spilt over her like everyone else. She's got a bigger television set than most people, I agree – but that'll be out of date in a few years' time. And, anyway, is a twenty-four-inch screen really worth selling your soul to the devil for – when your hairdresser probably gets a clearer picture on his seventeen?

HETTIE. *(mildly)* I didn't know you were so firmly right wing, Fiona.

FIONA. I'm not right wing. I'm on the side of the hairdresser, I think equality's a very good thing. *(Wistfully)* Only – it – well – does rather take the romance out of life. Oh, well, I'm going to have a swim.

(She goes to the railings right where her bathing-dress has been hanging out to dry.)

Oh Lord! Mummy's down there.

HETTIE. Where?

FIONA. By the pool. *(She puts the bathing-dress back.)* I'll have my swim later.

HETTIE. Why? Who's she with?

FIONA. No one. She's just sitting there.

(HETTIE looks up at FIONA.)

Well, if I go down I'll have to talk to her.

(HETTIE continues to look.)

I want a swim, not a conversation.

(The french windows are opened and MONA appears. She is an American lady of great wealth, indomitable gaiety and uncertain age.)

HETTIE. Hullo, Mona. We were – just talking about you.

MONA. That's no subject for children. Where the hell's Rose? The Antoninis are going—

HETTIE. She's down by the pool.

MONA. Doing what, for God's sake?

FIONA. Nothing. Just sitting there, musing. Musing on her vanished youth.

MONA. That's enough from you, young lady. One day your youth will vanish and we'll see how you like that.

FIONA. Gosh. I wish it would, this minute. I hate the beastly thing. I want to be at least forty-five and be able to say 'foolish boy' to all my lovers.

MONA. *(to* **HETTIE***)* She's got lovers, already?

HETTIE. Only in dreams. They all look like Armand Duval.

MONA. Who's he? A dish?

HETTIE. A dish of the period.

*(***MONA*** stares at her questioningly.)*

He's dead, Mona. Don't worry. Anyway, another girl got him. I'll cope with the Antoninis.

(She goes inside.)

MONA. You were kind about me?

FIONA. *(at the gramophone)* Very sympathetic.

MONA. *(at the railings right)* What's she doing down there? Really?

FIONA. *(indifferently)* I don't know. She's taken to doing that rather a lot lately.

(She has put a record of 'The Sleeping Princess' on the gramophone. It now begins to play.)

MONA. She hasn't even got a drink.

FIONA. Oh, that's out altogether now. The last doctor's put her on a very strict regime. He even says she might have to leave the south of France altogether and go to Switzerland, or somewhere.

MONA. Switzerland? That shouldn't happen to a dog.

(A young man, ADRIAN, momentarily appears at the french windows, holding cards.)

ADRIAN. Mona, for God's sake – are you quitting just because I've got four canastas for once?

MONA. All right, Adrian. Just coming.

(ADRIAN disappears.)

(To herself) He's hell, that one. He'll have to go.

(She suddenly takes in Fiona's age group, and adopts another tone.)

What I meant, Fiona, was—

FIONA. *(indifferently)* That's all right, Mona. I realized from the way he was behaving at dinner that quite soon he'd have to go.

MONA. Cute little child. So innocent and fresh, and unsullied and doesn't miss a goddam trick.

FIONA. *(sententiously)* You mustn't confuse innocence with ignorance, Mona.

MONA. I'll confuse what I like with what I like, see. As an adult that's my right.

(She smiles at FIONA and goes into the house. FIONA, listening to the music, does a couple of very ill-executed ballet steps. Then she picks up the recording machine, which is plainly quite a weight. RON appears on the steps left. He is dressed and coiffured a shade more soberly than when we last saw him, but this sobriety hardly extends, at the moment, to himself. He has plainly had quite a few drinks.)

FIONA. Hullo, Ron. I didn't know you were coming. Help me with this.

RON. *(doing so)* What is it?

FIONA. It's a recording machine. Mummy bought it for me to practise on – but I don't want her to know I've been using it, or she'll want to hear it, and then she'll be *kind*. Know what I mean?

RON. Who better?

FIONA. Thanks.

RON. This music for my benefit?

FIONA. No, but as you're here, you can jolly well do some work for your living. *(She gets into a ballet position.)* Come on.

RON. *(at drink table, pouring himself a drink)* No. Not tonight.

FIONA. Come on.

RON. I'm not in the mood. *(He knocks a glass over on the tray.)*

FIONA. You're drunk, that's what.

RON. I certainly am not.

FIONA. All right, then. Go on. Prove it.

> *(***RON*** puts his cigarette down and goes up to **FIONA**. He stands behind her, also adopting a ballet pose. **FIONA**, in her eagerness, begins a movement.)*

RON. No. Wait for the music. One, two, three – now. Arabesque.

> *(**FIONA** executes a very clumsy arabesque.)*

Another.

> *(**FIONA** does another, giggling with delight.)*

All right. Now. Allez-oops.

> *(He lifts her on to his shoulder with practised ease. Still giggling, she clutches first at his neck. Then she removes her hands precariously and waves her arms triumphantly in the air.)*

FIONA. No hands.

> *(***RON***, holding her firmly, executes a few turns, to the accompaniment of shrieks of delight from **FIONA**. Then he stops and lifts her to the ground, finishing the movement with a balletic flourish – on his knees, his left hand on his heart, his right directed towards **FIONA** in earnest homage.)*

Gosh! Oh, gosh, ballet's fun. Ron, do you think I could change my mind about R.A.D.A. and be a ballet dancer?

RON. *(taking up his cigarette)* No. You're too old. You have to start at about ten.

FIONA. Is that when you started?

RON. No. I started at eight.

FIONA. At eight. Gosh! You must have been keen.

RON. Yes, I was, then.

FIONA. Come on, Ron. Just once more.

RON. No.

FIONA. *(behind his chair, wheedling him)* Come on—

(**HETTIE** *comes out, and stops short at sight of* **RON.** *He does not get up.*)

RON. *(with a shade of defiance)* Good evening, Hettie.

HETTIE. *(with a shade of alarm)* Rose didn't ask you over tonight?

RON. No. Can't say she did. Just thought I'd drop by.

HETTIE. Without telephoning?

RON. Wanted to surprise her. Where is she?

HETTIE. *(quickly)* No idea.

(*She glances quickly and warningly at* **FIONA.** *The exchange is not lost on* **RON.**)

She's gone out somewhere.

RON. When will she be back?

HETTIE. I don't know.

RON. *(nodding at the house)* There are people in there.

HETTIE. Only Mona and Adrian.

RON. *(getting up)* Dear old Mona. I'll get a welcome from her at least.

(*He gets up and with slightly self-conscious effrontery walks past* **HETTIE** *into the house.*)

(*As he goes in.*) Hullo, Mona.

MONA. *(off)* Why, Ron. This is wonderful. Come and join us in a hand—

HETTIE. *(angrily, muttering)* The nerve. *(To* **FIONA,** *sternly.)* Fiona, I don't like you having anything to do with that character.

FIONA. Why not?

HETTIE. Because he's a bad boy.

FIONA. Do you think so? I think he's rather a sad boy – trying hard to be a bad boy. Anyway, why shouldn't I be polite to Mummy's friends?

HETTIE. *(for once nonplussed)* Your mother just happens to admire him as a dancer—

FIONA. Really? I didn't think she'd ever seen him dance. I have. He's good virtuoso – that's all. He hasn't the feeling to put him right up top. Pity, because he's got the technique. Is that what Mummy thinks?

HETTIE. *(after a pause.)* Lord, sixteen's an awkward age, isn't it? Still, it's not too old for spanking. You'd better go to bed before I get too tempted.

FIONA. No. I'm going up to the top of the hill. Only for ten minutes – but I want to rehearse that speech again.

HETTIE. Why not in your room?

FIONA. There's a statue of the Grand Duke Auguste up there. I speak the lines to him. He kind of inspires me. He's got the right period clothes, too.

(She goes out left. **HETTIE** *calls over the railings right.)*

HETTIE. Rose.

ROSE. *(off)* Yes?

HETTIE. Come up. There's a crisis.

ROSE. *(off)* Have we run out of vodka?

HETTIE. A lot worse than that. Come up quick. What in hell do you do down there anyway?

ROSE. *(off, nearer)* Cogitate.

HETTIE. Can't you cogitate when you haven't got guests? I had to say goodbye to the Antoninis for you.

(ROSE *appears, in evening dress.*)

ROSE. What a social disaster! I'll never be able to show my face in Cannes society again.

(*She begins to cough, and sits down. She seems exhausted by her climb from the pool.*)

(*Between coughs*) How much did they cheat at canasta tonight?

HETTIE. I don't know. I wasn't watching them.

(*She is, however, watching* ROSE, *as she coughs into a handkerchief. She pours out a glass of water and takes it to her.*)

ROSE. Thanks. It's those damn steps. I think I'll have a lift put in. (*Recovering herself*) Well, all right. Give me the crisis. It's about Ron, isn't it?

HETTIE. How do you know?

ROSE. You've got your Ron face on.

HETTIE. Have I got a Ron face?

ROSE. Like a disapproving Victorian governess. (*Cheerfully*) Well, what's he done this time? Smashed up the new car?

HETTIE. (*with sudden and surprising virulence*) I wish to God he had, and him with it.

ROSE. (*gently*) Now, now, Hettie. That's dangerous talk.

HETTIE. Oh no. He won't last.

ROSE. He might, you know. He just might.

(*She has taken a cigarette and now lights it.* HETTIE *looks at her.*)

This is allowed. Ten a day. My seventh. Well, go on. I can take it. What's he done?

HETTIE. Only turned up in this house tonight, uninvited and blotto.

ROSE. (*with quick eagerness*) He's here?

HETTIE. (*pointing to the sitting-room*) Playing canasta with Mona.

(Pause)

ROSE. Fancy him coming for once without being asked.

HETTIE. Fancy.

(ROSE has wandered to the sitting-room window and looks through it.)

ROSE. The cashmere jacket's rather a success, don't you think?

HETTIE. Great.

ROSE. The hair's fine, now, too, isn't it?

HETTIE. Fine.

(ROSE turns from the window and makes a move at HETTIE.)

ROSE. Oh well, better anyway.

(Until now she has plainly enjoyed the implications of HETTIE's news. Now her voice becomes hard and firm.)

All right. You'd better ring Kurt and tell him not to come up here for me. I'll meet him down at Maxim's at twelve-thirty.

HETTIE. I can't. He's dining at St. Tropez. I don't know where, and anyway he's probably on his way by now.

ROSE. Yes, of course. *(She looks at her watch.)* Well, I've got plenty of time. Get Ron out here, will you?

HETTIE. Away from Mona?

ROSE. Yes.

(HETTIE turns. ROSE suddenly runs after her and catches her arm.)

Why that voice? Are you trying to make mischief?

HETTIE. Yes.

ROSE. All right. Give it to me. What do you know?

HETTIE. Only what you know. That he went to Mona's party on Thursday without letting you know, and the tobacco shares that Mona's last husband left her are paying pretty well this year. Better than an actor's alimony which he defaults on every month anyway – plus the odd present from Kurt. If you want to keep a Ron, you should have husbands that die, like Mona's.

(Pause)

ROSE. Please don't hate him so much, Hettie. For my sake, don't hate him so much.

HETTIE. For your sake, I'd do a lot of things. That, no.

(ROSE turns away with a shrug.)

ROSE. *(smiling)* I happen to know he tried to call me Thursday—

HETTIE. Who do you happen to know it from?

(Pause)

ROSE. Go and get him – there's a dear. Play his cards for him. Mona won't mind.

(HETTIE nods and goes into the sitting-room. ROSE turns eagerly at first to face the french windows and then as RON'S shadow appears, hastily turns away from the house, as if gazing unconcernedly at the view. RON goes up to her and kisses her on the back of the neck. She takes his hand.)

RON. Had you really gone out, or was that old bitch lying as usual?

ROSE. She was lying as usual. I was in the garden.

RON. Alone?

ROSE. Yes.

RON. Thinking of me?

ROSE. Amongst other things.

(She turns and kisses him on the lips. On neither side is the embrace very passionate; affectionate on hers, and on his rather balletically romantic. Then ROSE pushes him away and looks at his jacket appraisingly.)

ROSE. Yes. It's very good. Suits you wonderfully.

RON. Bit too much on the shoulders. They can't cut in France. I'm taking it back. I don't want to look like a spiv, do I?

ROSE. No.

(RON *goes to the drink tray and pours himself a drink.* ROSE *watches him.*)

RON. Want one?

ROSE. No. I'm off it. Doctor's orders.

RON. Good girl.

ROSE. *(a shade timidly)* Do you think you should, Ron? You've had a few tonight, haven't you?

RON, *(with sudden ferocity)* Don't mother me. I hate being mothered— *(He downs his glass of rosé.)*

ROSE. I was only thinking of your dancing.

RON. I know exactly what you were thinking of.

ROSE. *(after a pause)* It really *was* your performance on the stage I was worrying about, Ron.

(Pause. RON, *without replying, pours himself out another rosé. Then he turns and flashes* ROSE *a beaming smile.*)

RON. This stuff's like water, you know. Couldn't hurt a fly.

ROSE. Ron, dear, I'm terribly sorry, but I'm afraid I'll have to ask you to leave in a minute.

RON. Leave?

ROSE. I've got Kurt coming up quite soon and I'm going out with him.

RON. I see.

ROSE. He goes on his yacht tomorrow for a two months' trip. This is his last night in Cannes and I can't put him off tonight. I really can't. Any other night – but not this.

RON. I see.

ROSE. You should have phoned.

RON. Wouldn't have made much difference if I had, would it? – except it might have saved me some petrol.

ROSE. *(unhappily)* I'm sorry, Ron.

RON. I wanted like hell to see you tonight.

ROSE. *(tenderly)* Did you, Ron? Well – tomorrow—

RON. I wanted tonight. Anyway, I've got my suitcase in the car and I need a bed.

ROSE. *(after a pause)* You've had a row with Sam?

RON. It was bound to come, wasn't it?

ROSE. Was it about me?

RON. Well, indirectly. I think it was really about the new car—

ROSE. Indirectly, I suppose that might have been about me.

RON. It showed up his – that was the trouble – and he just couldn't bear it. He just couldn't. Anyway, I'm glad it's over. He's done three of our ballets this season, and I've had the lead in two of them – not the last one – oh no – that came after you, so I didn't get that one – that little creep Michel Bran got that – but anyway people in the company were beginning to talk and I was being made to feel a bit – I don't know – cheap.

ROSE. *(laughing quietly)* Oh, but that's the last thing you ever ought to feel, Ron.

(RON *looks at her, then walks quickly up to her and takes her hand.*)

RON. *(fiercely)* Listen, Saturday night, you said something to me – remember?

ROSE. I said a lot of things to you.

RON. One thing in particular.

ROSE. *(after a pause)* I said I was very fond of you.

RON. Was that true?

(Pause)

ROSE. *(quietly)* Yes, Ron. Quite true.

RON. So you're very fond of me. So why are you always needling me, sending me up, taking the mickey out of me? Why? Why? *(Shaking her)* Why do you needle me?

ROSE. It's not you I needle, Ron. It's myself.

RON. That's another thing. You talk in a lot of bloody riddles to me – all the time – sometimes like you were just talking to yourself just to make yourself laugh. Ce n'est pas trés chic, ça, je t'assure.

ROSE. *(with an affectionate smile.)* Non, chéri. Je suis de ton avis. G'est une habitude abominable. Je te demande pardon.

RON. Did you ever take French lessons?

ROSE. *(laughing)* Yes. From records, in Edgbaston. My first husband bought them for me. I thought they might come in handy some time. They did. When he died and left me two thousand I came down here and captured myself a French husband. Is that another thing you're going to hold against me – that I speak French better than you?

RON. It doesn't help. It doesn't help that you do everything better than me—

ROSE. Give yourself time, Ron. Remember you're only just starting.

(**MONA** *appears at the window.*)

MONA. Hi. How long are you going to monopolize this guy? I've got fifty dollars to get back yet—

ROSE. I told Hettie to take his hand.

MONA. Hell. I don't play with Hettie. She's too goddam good.

RON. All right, Mona, I'll be with you in a second.

(**MONA**, *sensing an atmosphere, turns to the window.*)

MONA. You better.

(*She disappears.*)

RON. What time's Kurt coming for you?

ROSE. Twelve.

RON. O.K. You tip me the wink when you hear the car, and I'll nip upstairs. End room?

ROSE. No.

RON. *(turning on his way to the door)* No?

ROSE. No. I don't want you in this house tonight. I'll get Hettie to book you a room at the Carlton. Tomorrow you can come up here.

(RON, *without saying anything, or even appearing to have heard, goes to the drink tray and pours himself a rosé.*)

(*Looking at her watch*) And don't play more than one hand with Mona. Try and get out by ten to twelve—

(RON *looks at her, clicks his heels and salutes.*)

RON. Yes, ma'am. Very good, ma'am.

ROSE. (*ignoring the pantomime*) And as I may not see you to say goodnight, I'd like to say it now. Also to thank you for coming all this way to see me.

(*She goes to him and kisses him, as before, with warmth but without passion.*)

RON. (*bowing now and clicking his heels*) Your ladyship's most bloody humble and bloodiest possible obedient servant.

(*He turns to the sitting-room, stumbling as he does so.*)

ROSE. (*quickly*) Ron.

(*He turns.*)

You *did* try and phone me Thursday, didn't you?

RON. Thursday?

ROSE. The night of Mona's party.

RON. Oh. Yes, of course I did. I told you. My phone was out of order.

ROSE. (*quickly*) You said *mine* was.

(*Pause*)

RON. (*shrugging*) Yours – mine. Anybody caring?

ROSE. Nobody that matters much.

RON. (*feeling he may have gone too far*) Now, Rose, my dearest Rose – you can't possibly think—

ROSE. Go back to your canasta, Ron. Only one hand. Double the stakes, if you like. I'll pay your losses.

(*Pause.* RON *stares at her, half angry, half frightened.*)

RON. Your Majesty's generosity knows no bounds.

(*He gives her an elaborate bow, as to a ballet queen, and then makes an exit into the sitting-room in full ballet style – hoping, evidently, to make Rose laugh. She does not. The moment he has gone, she goes quickly to the drink tray and, with slightly feverish hands, pours herself a brandy. She is squirting soda into the glass as* HETTIE *comes in.*)

ROSE. (*raising her glass*) Caught red-handed. This isn't the last either. Back to the regime tomorrow.

HETTIE. What's upset you?

ROSE. Who knows better than you, you wicked old pudding-stirrer.

HETTIE. Scene about Mona?

ROSE. No. But nearly. My God, how nearly. (*To herself, in wonderment*) Me – jealous! Jealous – of Mona! God! You may be right, Hettie. Perhaps I'd better call time.

HETTIE. (*morosely*) If it's not too late.

ROSE. Too late? Of course it's not too late. I could give him up tomorrow if I wanted to.

HETTIE. Why don't you want to?

ROSE. (*after a pause*) Maybe it's just that at my late age I'm getting a bit bored with always being the loved one. Maybe I'm beginning to feel it's time that *I* did the loving.

HETTIE. (*scornfully*) Loving!

ROSE. (*after a pause*) Yes. In a way – loving. You mustn't confuse me with Mona.

HETTIE. If you behave like her, how can I avoid it?

ROSE. Fair comment. (*With a smile*) Oh Lord, how can I explain it? It's not *that,* anyway. At least not very much – not nearly enough to justify that nasty word

that's trembling on those Victorian lips. I don't give
him cashmere jackets and Lagondas just to get him to
bed, Hettie. I think I can do that without – I really do –
and I'm not one to flatter myself on that score, as you
know. No, I give him cashmere jackets and Lagondas
for the simple and honest reason that I enjoy giving
him cashmere jackets and Lagondas. It's fun to give.
Great fun. I never really knew how much. You see,
I haven't had much practice in it until now.

HETTIE. Have you had a look at the accounts lately—?

ROSE. Don't be so materialistic, Hettie. All right. So the
Lagonda was a mistake, and so I'll never be able to pay
for it, without selling a couple of pictures. But that's
not all I give him, and enjoy giving him. *(Musingly)*
He's a bit lost, our Ron, you know. Of course he
doesn't realize it. Oh no— *(imitating)* he knows his
way through the jungle – knows it like the back of his
hand. Well, I've been through the same jungle myself,
in my time, and quite frankly, Hettie, I don't think the
poor little brute even knows the back of his hand. Yes.
It's rather fun hacking a path for him without his even
knowing it.

HETTIE. You must be very happy then to see that the path
you've hacked for him has led straight to a clearing
called Mona.

(Pause. ROSE gets up and goes to the drink tray.)

ROSE. Yes. All right. One up.

HETTIE. Don't have another brandy. Have a vin rosé.

ROSE. I prefer a woman's drink, thank you. *(She pours herself
a brandy and soda.) Yes.* You're right. He'll have to go.
I can't have my heart skipping a couple of beats at the
sound of another woman's name. Not yet, anyway. Not
at thirty-five. Not until I have to. Oh yes – he'll have to
go, all right – the poor little beast—

(FIONA comes in left.)

Hullo, darling. I didn't know you'd gone out.

HETTIE. I told her she could. I thought you wouldn't mind.

ROSE. Of course I don't mind. I don't know why you two always behave as if I was an ogress-mother.

HETTIE. Well – you've been known to fuss.

ROSE. Only about her health. She's very delicate. She doesn't look after herself as she should—

HETTIE. Pardon a slight titter.

ROSE. That's different. *I'm* tough. When I was her age I was fighting girls in Frogmore Road twice her size. And beating them. Did you have a nice time tonight, darling?

FIONA. *(politely)* Yes, thank you, Mummy. I'm going to bed now. Good night. *(She goes towards the french windows.)*

ROSE. *(timidly, as always with Fiona)* Fiona – I met David Cranston at Eden Roc this afternoon.

FIONA. *(excitedly)* David Cranston? He's down here? Isn't he up at Stratford?

ROSE. He's got a week off.

FIONA. Oh, Mummy, what's he like to talk to? Does he speak right down in his boots like he does on the stage? Is he very good-looking?

ROSE. *(complacently)* Well, you'll have a chance of finding out all that tomorrow afternoon, because he's coming up here.

*(The effect of the news on **FIONA** is not at all as evidently envisaged by **ROSE**. The smile is wiped off **FIONA**'s face and her eyes narrow suspiciously.)*

FIONA. Up here?

ROSE. Yes. And just to meet you. I told him all about you and your ambitions. He was very interested—

FIONA. Oh Mummy, of course he wasn't interested—

ROSE. He was, you know. He even said he'd hear you read a part—

FIONA. *(with some force)* No.

ROSE. You mustn't be scared, darling.

FIONA. I'm not scared, but I won't let him hear me read. Not up here, where he's your guest and has to be polite.

ROSE. It's a wonderful chance.

FIONA. Of course it is, but I won't do it. I won't. One day I'll read to him on a stage, when I'll just be Fiona Hawkins and one of fifty others and he won't know whose daughter I am. But not until.

ROSE. *(quietly)* But he *will* know whose daughter you are, won't he – as you're going to meet him tomorrow?

(FIONA shakes her head.)

You mean, you don't want even to meet him?

(FIONA shakes her head again, plainly deeply disturbed.)

But he's your favourite of all, isn't he?

FIONA. I once waited in the rain for an hour outside the Haymarket to get his autograph – and then I missed it. But I'm not going to meet him up here. I'm sorry, Mummy. I'll go out tomorrow—

ROSE. But it was entirely for your sake that I asked him, darling—

FIONA. Yes, Mummy. I know that. I'm awfully sorry.

ROSE. *(growing angry)* But why, for heaven's sake?

FIONA. I can't explain it. I only know I don't want to meet him if he's coming up here to have a drink with you.

(Pause)

ROSE. *(quietly)* You say some hurting things sometimes, Fiona.

FIONA. If I do, I don't mean them.

ROSE. No. I don't think you do. That doesn't stop them from hurting.

FIONA. I'm sorry, Mummy. May I go to bed now?

ROSE. Yes. You should.

(FIONA walks dutifully over to ROSE and plants a filial kiss on her cheek.)

FIONA. Good night, Mummy.

ROSE. Good night, Fiona.

FIONA. Good night, Hettie.

HETTIE. Good night, you little beast.

FIONA. *You* understand, don't you?

HETTIE. Don't drag me into it. Go on.

(*FIONA goes into the house.*)

ROSE. *Do* you understand?

HETTIE. *(tactfully)* Not really.

ROSE. You do, I think. What is it? She can't dislike me all that much, can she?

HETTIE. Of course she doesn't dislike you. All she dislikes is being the daughter of Rose Fish.

ROSE. But Rose Fish doesn't shock her. I know it doesn't—

HETTIE. I know, too. But there's a difference between not being shocked by Rose Fish and wanting to be Rose Fish's daughter.

ROSE. *(shrugging)* The wages of sin?

HETTIE. Part of them. Not a very important part, I'd say.

ROSE. *(with sudden violence)* God, Hettie. The most important part. I'd give anything – anything in the world – to break down the defences of that remote, withdrawn little monster, and make her feel something for me. Something. Even shame or hatred. I could cope with that. What I can't cope with is 'Yes, Mummy', 'No Mummy', 'I'm sorry, Mummy', 'May I go to bed, Mummy'. Oh God, Hettie, if only I could get her to *need* me.

HETTIE. The wail of mothers all down the centuries.

ROSE. *(wiping her eyes quickly)* This mother happens to be rather a special mother – and means it rather specially—

HETTIE. That's the first time I've ever seen you cry.

ROSE. It's just about the first time I ever have. Damn it! How idiotic! I don't know why she dislikes being the daughter of Rose Fish. If you ask me she's damn lucky to be the daughter of Rose Fish.

HETTIE. I cordially agree.

(There is the sound of a car drawing up, and headlights light up the railings left.)

ROSE. Oh God, Kurt. *(Looking at her watch)* Quarter of an hour early. Trust him. *(Coolly)* I'll keep him here for a few minutes. You get Ron out of the house. Book him a room at the Carlton – charge it to me. Tell him to call after his rehearsal tomorrow and come over for supper if he wants to.

HETTIE. He'll want to.

ROSE. And tell him to bring his things. From tomorrow he's staying here. *(Calling into drive)* Hullo, Kurt. Come on up on the terrace.

HETTIE. I thought you said he had to go.

ROSE. I'll think about that tomorrow. Go on.

(HETTIE goes. After a moment KURT appears. He is in a white dinner jacket.)

You're early.

KURT. I know. The most boring party. Disgusting food, and all trying to play me for crazy schemes like I was the biggest sucker in Europe. *(He stops and looks at her appraisingly.)* Yes. You are looking good tonight. Very good.

(He kisses her slowly and with evident relish. She accepts the embrace composedly.)

ROSE. *(emerging at length)* You've ruined my make-up.

KURT. Not *your* make-up, my dear. It can stand up to more than that. It has to, I'd guess.

ROSE. Not unless *you're* around – you wolf.

KURT. *(laughing)* You are being in good form tonight. That is good. We will be having fun tonight, my baby. We will be beating up this old burg tonight like it has not been beaten in ions.

ROSE. *(correcting)* Aeons.

KURT. Aeons? So? I was reading it today for the first time. It's a good word. It means for ever, like the way I love you. Your guests have gone?

ROSE. No. Mona and her boy friend are still here.

KURT. Not the boy friend, my dear. When I was coming in the drive, he was leaving it – going like the goddam wind.

ROSE. Oh? He and Mona must have had one of their tiffs. She wasn't with him?

KURT. No. Go and say good-bye to her and then we shoot off— *(He turns to go back to the car.)*

ROSE. *(coolly)* Just a moment, Kurt.

(He turns.)

You know I hate talking sordid business matters late at night.

KURT. Quite right, my dear. Late at night is most unsuitable.

(He takes out a cheque book and a pen. He deliberately opens it on a table and poises the pen over a cheque. One feels he enjoys the moment.)

O.K. Baby. Shoot.

ROSE. I honestly don't know how much we're owing at the moment. I'm afraid it's rather a lot. I'll have to ask Hettie—

KURT. *(beginning to write)* No need to be asking Hettie. This will be round enough for any owings—

ROSE. *(automatically correcting)* Debts.

KURT. Debts. As if that word I should know.

(He hands her a cheque. She glances at it.)

ROSE. *(quietly, handing it back)* No, I won't need all that. Thanks all the same, but make it for half, would you?

KURT. *(putting his arm around her gleefully)* My baby, my baby, to whom are you saying that? And who is saying it to me? Make it for half! Yes, you are being in good form tonight.

ROSE. *(putting the cheque into her bag)* I meant it, you know. You're too generous.

KURT. I am a business man. Value for money. For the best goods you must always be paying the highest prices—

(**ROSE** *turns abruptly to the drink tray and pours herself a brandy.*)

Can't you wait until Maxim's?

ROSE. Frankly, no. *(She turns and lifts the glass to him.)* Thank you, Kurt. I'm very grateful.

KURT. *(deprecatingly)* My dear—

ROSE. The gambling's been terrible lately, and a lot of expenses seem to have come all at once. Decorating this house, and fixing up the pool—

KURT. *(quietly)* And buying a Lagonda for Ron Vale—

(**ROSE** *stares at him in silence. He laughs delightedly.*)

My dear, when other people are saying they have spies everywhere, they are using an expression of speaking. But with Kurt Mast it may not be such nonsense talk.

(**ROSE** *opens her bag and takes out the cheque. She walks over to him. As she reaches him he pushes her outstretched hand impatiently away from him.*)

KURT. Don't be crazy. Do you think I am caring?

ROSE. *(quietly)* But you should care, shouldn't you?

KURT. About a Ron Vale? My dearest honey child, I am hearing my baby has found herself a little ballet boy, and I am saying not my baby, not my Rose, such things are not for her – a Greek shipowner, yes, but not a ballet boy. And then I am finding out it is goddam true. But I am also checking up on this Vale – Valof, and baby. *(He laughs.)* Oh well, I am saying, if my Rose, who I am always knowing is so generous and so extravagant is wanting to throw money away by giving expensive motor-cars to such a boy – well, I am not objecting. Not yet. When she is my wife – another story. Also when I see this Vale I will very likely be pulling him apart with my hands. But caring? Me? About such a boy. Pfui. *My* Rose is still *my* Rose and no one else's and I am knowing it goddam well.

(Pause. **ROSE** *tears up the cheque deliberately, and puts the pieces in an ashtray.)*

Why so dramatic? Don't you know I will only be writing you another one later?

ROSE. Yes. You certainly will.

KURT. *(laughing)* For double, to punish me?

ROSE, No. For exactly this amount – less the price of a Lagonda.

KURT. I am not knowing the price of a Lagonda.

ROSE. Nor am I exactly, but we'll find out. Now let's go. I'll just get my wrap—

(Her voice fades as **RON** *appears at the sitting-room windows. He is drunker than when last seen.)*

RON. I just came to tell you that you don't need to worry about a bed for me tonight. Mona's going to put me up. *(Turning to* **KURT**) Good evening, Herr Mast. We met once before, do you remember? You thought I was a journalist.

KURT. Yes. I remember.

RON. You told me you had no objection to the expression 'Gutter tycoon' and I'm glad about that. Very glad, because you see I think it's a very good expression indeed— 'Gutter tycoon'. Very good.

ROSE. *(authoritatively)* Go and say hullo to Mona and Hettie, would you, Kurt?

*(***KURT*** *stands for a moment undecided, then turns briskly to the window and goes into the house without looking back.)*

Trying to get yourself killed, Ron?

RON. Let him have a go. I'd be only too happy.

ROSE. He doesn't have to do it himself, you know. He's got plenty of thugs around.

RON. Nice class of people you choose for your boy friends, don't you?

ROSE. Yes, I do, don't I? All right. The damage is done now. You'd better go in the End Room.

RON. I've told you. I'm not going in the End Room, or the Carlton, or any other damn place. I'm staying with Mona.

(Pause)

ROSE. How drunk are you, Ron?

RON. Not so drunk I don't know exactly what I'm doing.

ROSE. You know that if you stay with Mona tonight, you'll never see me again.

RON. Yes, I know that. One law for the bloody rich and another for the bloody poor. You can go off on the town with your gutter tycoon, but I have to be a good little boy and tuck myself up in the Carlton – probably with Hettie locking me in.

ROSE. I'm sorry, Ron, but I'm just telling you the facts. I'm not discussing the justice of them.

RON. All right – so you've told me the facts.

ROSE. And you accept them?

RON. You bet I accept them. I bloody well welcome them.

ROSE. All right. So that's it. *(Smiling at him)* How do we say goodbye in a situation like this? It's rather difficult to know. Shake hands and wish each other luck?

RON. Fish. God, they knew something when they gave you that name. Do you breathe with gills? Have you any feelings at all? Have you ever given one minute's thought to me in the last two months?

ROSE. Yes, Ron. Quite a few minutes.

RON. I wonder. Have you ever thought what it's been like for me, asked over here a couple of odd evenings a week whenever there're no important people around – because common Ron mustn't meet important people – oh dear no – that'd never do – and then when I'm here shoved around, needled, sent up – everyone talking about people I don't know, and things I don't understand. Do you know why I came over tonight? Do you know?

ROSE. To get a bed, I thought.

RON. I could have got a hundred beds without driving for an hour and a half. I came over to find out what sort of greeting I'd get from my girl if I turned up here out of the blue without letting her know. A kind of test case you could call it. Well, I found out all right. My God, I found out. The paid companion is sent in to bundle me out of the house because the other boy friend – the rich one – has turned up unexpectedly—

ROSE. *(wearily)* Oh, really, Ron. You've always known about Kurt—

RON. And has that made it any easier, do you think? Do you think I enjoy living on your immoral earnings?

ROSE. You mean you'd rather they were moral earnings? Like Mona's tobacco shares?

RON. That's right. Be funny. Make a joke. Needle me. My feelings don't matter a damn, and never have.

(Pause. ROSE goes up to him, at length, and gives him an affectionate kiss.)

ROSE. Goodbye, Ron.

(HETTIE comes in and stands in the window.)

HETTIE. *(to ROSE)* Having any trouble?

ROSE. No. No trouble at all.

(She goes into the house.)

RON. I suppose you're pleased about this.

HETTIE. Delighted.

RON. *(pouring himself a rosé)* And so am I. My God, am I delighted? I feel free now, my own master, and it's a good feeling.

HETTIE. I wonder if Mona will appreciate the feeling.

RON. Listen, if you think I'm going to jump out of *this* frying-pan into *that* fire, you're wrong. Dead wrong. When I say free, I mean free.

HETTIE. Going to give back the Lagonda?

RON. Who knows?

HETTIE. I do, I think.

RON. You're not as wise as you like to believe, Hettie, I might surprise you.

HETTIE. You might, but will you?

RON. *(bravely)* All right. Send to Monte tomorrow and collect it. There. Or do you want it in writing?

HETTIE. Oh no. Your word, I'm sure, is your bond.

(**ROSE** *comes on to the terrace, now with wrap, talking quite gaily to* **MONA.** **KURT** *follows them.*)

ROSE. No, it's red, impair and my age tonight. At chemmy, it's bancos. The banks won't run.

MONA. Famous last words. What's it for you, Kurt?

KURT. Baccarat.

ROSE. It's always baccarat for Kurt, and he always wins.

KURT. Because I am lucky in love.

ROSE. It's the other way round, darling.

MONA. I've a good mind to come down with you.

ROSE. Why don't you?

MONA. What about it, Ron?

RON. I've got to be early tonight. I'm dancing tomorrow.

KURT. What are you dancing tomorrow?

RON. The Blue Bird.

KURT. The blue bird? What is that? You have wires and go flying over the stage – like Peter Pansy?

(He flutters his arms in a derisory gesture.)

RON. *(quietly)* No. Not like Peter Pansy. The Blue Bird is a virtuoso part, and I'd say just about as difficult to dance well as to make a fortune out of the black market—

ROSE. You won't come then, Mona? *(To* **KURT***)* All right, darling. Then let's go.

*(**FIONA** comes in in a dressing-gown.)*

FIONA. I'm going to have a swim, Mummy.

ROSE. You ought to be asleep, Fiona.

FIONA. Swimming helps me to sleep. I do it every night.

(*She moves towards the steps and collects her bathing-suit.*)

KURT. I must come to Monte Carlo one night, Mr. Vale, and see you dancing these virtuoso dances that are so difficult—

RON. Don't bother, Herr Mast. Monte Carlo is a long way and from what you told me about yourself the other morning I doubt if you appreciate the fine arts very much. I tell you what. I'll give you an exhibition now. (*Rounding on* **FIONA**) Here's my partner.

FIONA. No, Ron. Not now.

RON. Nonsense. (*To* **ROSE**) You haven't seen us do this, have you, Rose?

FIONA. No, Ron, please. We haven't any music.

RON. Who wants music—

(*He gets into ballet position behind her.*)

FIONA. No, Ron.

RON. Now don't be scared. What have you got to be scared of? (*He begins to hum the music of 'Swan Lake'.*) Now, Arabesque.

(**FIONA** *obediently performs, plainly not enjoying herself.*)

Well done. Now another.

(*She does it again.*)

Bravo. You have a budding Fonteyn here. Now— allez-oops. (*He lifts* **FIONA** *on to his shoulder.*)

HETTIE. (*quietly*) Ron – stop it.

RON. What about that? Isn't she marvellous? Now hold tight, and we'll show them a bit of virtuoso stuff.

HETTIE. No, Ron. Let her down.

RON. (*to* **FIONA**) All right? Here we go, then.

(He does a spectacular turn, successful the first time, but in repeating it, trips and falls. FIONA screams. RON twists his body around so as to fall backwards and break FIONA'S fall.)

ROSE. Oh, my God! *(Running to FIONA's side)* Fiona, are you all right?

FIONA. *(scrambling to her feet)* Yes, Mummy. I think so. *(She feels her elbow)* Bit of a bump here, that's all.

HETTIE. Let's see. *(She examines FIONA's elbow.)*

KURT. *(also looking at it)* A bruise tomorrow, maybe. *(To HETTIE)* The best thing is a hot compress—

FIONA. Oh no. It's not bad at all. Just hurts a bit.

MONA. If s the funny bone, I expect. That always hurts.

(RON, meanwhile, unwatched by anyone, has been lying motionless on the ground. He now gets laboriously to his feet. As he puts his right ankle to the ground it crumples under him and, as he straightens it, we can see that he is in great pain. He nevertheless manages to stand, nonchalantly holding on to a chair.)

RON. I'm sorry, Fiona.

FIONA. That's all right.

RON. I'm a lousy partner. Always have been. Much better alone and that's the truth.

ROSE. *(to FIONA)* Better go to bed, darling. Hettie'll look after you.

FIONA. Yes, Mummy. *(ROSE kisses her.)* Good night. Good night, everyone. Good night, Ron. It wasn't your fault. I overbalanced—

(She goes out, followed by HETTIE.)

MONA. You've got your car, Ron?

RON. Yes.

MONA. I'll go ahead, then. You know the way?

RON. Like the back of my hand.

(ROSE looks at him for about the first time, and what she sees in his motionless form tells her the truth.)

MONA. *(on her way out)* Good night, Rose darling. Lovely evening.

ROSE. *(accepting her kiss, still looking at* RON*)* Glad you enjoyed it, Mona.

*(*MONA *goes out.)*

KURT. Well, I have much enjoyed your exhibition of this virtuoso dancing, Mr Vale. And that is as difficult to perform as to make five hundred million marks?

RON. We can all of us come an unexpected cropper, Herr Mast. Let's face it – any of us back-street boys can sometimes make bad.

(Barely perceptibly he staggers, and holds on tightly to the chair.)

ROSE. *(to* KURT*)* Darling, go on to Maxim's, will you? I'm a bit worried about Fiona and she might need a doctor or something. I'll use my car. *(As* KURT *is about to protest)* Order me Lanson '47 and scrambled eggs. I'll be down in ten minutes.

KURT. I would not be liking it to be any longer.

ROSE. It won't be. Don't forget the Lanson '47, or they'll try and palm you off with a non-vintage. And no nonsense about caviar aux blinis. Just scrambled eggs—

KURT. *(at steps)* Good night, Mr. Vale – and I think I am meaning goodbye, is it not?

RON, *(wearily)* Yes, it may be, Herr Mast. God! this is a silly game – but I'll go on playing it if you like. Goodbye is a word that sounds very sweet when it's said to you.

ROSE. *(to* KURT *as he is about to reply)* Go on, Kurt. He's quite right, it's a silly game.

KURT. He may find, one day – silly or not – it is perhaps not such a game.

(He goes out. The second he is out of sight, RON *collapses on to his knees.)*

ROSE. *(authoritatively)* Lie down. Right down. On your back. That's right. *(She examines his ankle.)* Yes. It's broken.

RON. No. It's only a sprain.

ROSE. It's broken.

RON. What do you know about ankles?

ROSE. I was in the A.R.P. in the war. You damn little idiot. You've made it much worse getting up and standing on it.

RON. I wasn't going to give that Nazi bastard a belly laugh by seeing me down and out.

ROSE. Lie there. Don't move it any more whatever you do. I'll get a cushion for it.

(*She goes to collect a cushion,* **HETTIE** *comes in.*)

Hettie, ring up Doctor Marton and tell him to come up at once. Ron has broken his ankle.

RON. Sprained.

ROSE. Broken. There's no doubt, I'm afraid.

HETTIE. I'm sorry.

RON. (*wearily*) You're not, you old bitch, so why do you say so?

HETTIE. A perfect gentleman, isn't he? Even adversity he wears with a smile—

ROSE. Doctor Marton's number is in my book, Hettie.

(**HETTIE** *goes out.* **ROSE,** *kneeling beside* **RON,** *very gingerly lifts his leg a few inches and slips a cushion under his ankle.* **RON** *groans.*)

(*On the ground beside him*) I'm sorry, darling, but it's better that way.

(**RON** *suddenly grabs* **ROSE** *and buries his face in her stomach.*)

RON. (*sobbing*) Oh Rose! Oh my God!

ROSE. (*stroking his head*) Does it hurt very much?

RON. It hurt like hell when I was standing on it. It doesn't hurt now.

ROSE. Well, just stay quiet.

RON. (*with another sob*) Oh God!

ROSE. What is it, darling?

RON. It's so awful.

ROSE. It'll mend all right, Ron.

RON. I'm not talking about the bloody ankle. I'm talking
about me. About you and me. You all think I'm a
proper bastard, I know, and just out for what I can get,
and I dare say you may be right. But that's how I was
told when I was a kid – in this world, Ron boy, they
said, you got to work it so it's 'F.U., Jack, I'm all right',
or you go under – and Christ, Rose, that's true. Look
at the people who do go under – even in this bloody
Welfare world.

(*He raises a tear-stained face and looks up at her. She
says nothing, looking down at him, and continuing
mechanically to stroke his hair.*)

What's so wrong in looking after oneself? You've done
it all your life, haven't you?

ROSE. Yes.

RON. Why does everybody think I'm such a bastard because
I do it?

ROSE. Perhaps they think the same of me.

RON. They don't. You know that's a lie. (*Sobbing again*)
I can't give you up, you know. It's no good. I can
pretend about Mona. but she makes me bloody sick,
and Sam, and all the others. It's the same with them.
I can't give you up, Rose. Don't send me away.

(**ROSE** *does not reply. There is a pause.* **RON** *recovers
himself a little.*)

You think this is just another act, because I don't want
to lose my rich girl friend. Yes, I know that's the way
your mind works. I don't blame you. So would mine
in your place. Yes, all right. That's the way it started.
'Rose Fish? Oh yes, I know her very well. As a matter of
fact I'm popping up to the Chateau Auguste tomorrow
– staying all night as it happens. Yes, she's really very
nice – not a bit like what the papers say about her –
can't trust the papers, can you? – yes, awfully amusing,

and terribly beautiful – and, of course – mad about me—'

(He holds her tightly to him again.)

But it isn't like that now, Rose. I don't know just what's happened, but it isn't like that. Christ, I'm jealous of Kurt. Me! Jealous! What a laugh! *(He begins to sob again.)* I don't understand it. I hardly ever see you, when you call me in the mornings, we don't say much to each other, just gossip, your friends treat me like dirt and so do you, only more polite, and yet I can't damn well do without you. I need you in my life.

(He looks up at her again.)

For some bloody silly reason which I can't explain, I need you in my life.

(He is still looking at her waiting for some answer, when **HETTIE** *comes in.)*

HETTIE. Doctor Marton's on his way. I've also rung the hospital and got an ambulance.

ROSE. Thank you, Hettie. You've done very well. In a few moments would you ring Maxim's and tell Kurt that I'm not coming down tonight?

HETTIE. Shall I tell him what's happened?

ROSE. No.

HETTIE. Then what *shall* I tell him?

ROSE. Whatever you think best, in the circumstances.

HETTIE. What are the circumstances?

ROSE. I'm needed by Ron.

(She bends her head over **RON'S** *in a protective embrace.)*

(Curtain)

ACT TWO

Scene One

(Scene: The same, two months later.)

*(Five people sit on the terrace, with **ROSE** pouring coffee and giving the cups to **RON** to hand round. **RON** walks with a stick. The new face is that of **SAM DUVEEN**, a lean athletic-looking man in the middle forties. It is just after lunch.)*

ROSE. *(handing a cup to **RON**)* That's for Hettie. You shouldn't be doing this. Go and sit down—

RON. It's all right. He said as long as I don't put any weigh on it, it's all right.

ROSE. Fiona, you come and take coffee round, would you?

RON. *(taking the cup to **HETTIE**)* You all behave as if I'd done it yesterday. Dammit, it's been out of plaster since last week.

SAM. Ron's quite right, Mrs. Bradford. The more exercise he gives it, the sooner he'll be dancing again.

RON. I'm not dancing again.

*(He sits down. **SAM** looks at him in surprise.)*

ROSE. *(giving a cup to **FIONA**)* For Mr Duveen.

SAM. Not ever?

RON. No. I thought you knew.

SAM. You didn't tell me.

RON. I told everyone else, including the boss. I suppose I was scared to tell you, because I knew what you'd say.

ROSE. And what do you say, Mr. Duveen?

SAM. *(lightly)* Nothing at all. Why should I?

ROSE. *(a shade defensively)* It was his idea, you know. Not mine.

SAM. Oh, I'm quite sure of that.

ROSE. On the other hand I can't say I'm not glad. I didn't particularly relish the thought of being a dancer's wife and trekking all over Europe with him on one-night stands and things—

SAM. *(politely)* I quite agree. I don't know any dancer's wife who doesn't want her husband to give up the ballet.

RON. The trouble is it's the worst paid job in the world— and after years of sweating to get to the top you suddenly find you've had it because your muscles don't work so well any more. I ask you – what sort of career is it for anyone that ends at forty – without a pension?

SAM. Yes. It's a bad career, unless you happen to love it.

RON. And I never did. You know that. Remember how I used to shock you?

SAM. You did – but then about ballet I'm easily shockable.

ROSE. Was he good, Mr. Duveen?

SAM. As a technician, yes – but to have been good by the highest standards he needed to have worked a good deal harder than he did.

RON. Hell, Sam, I worked. I never missed class—

SAM. *(smiling)* Only because I told the boss to dock your pay cheque if you did. Besides, there's more in working at dancing than just not missing class.

ROSE. *(brightly)* Anyway, Mr. Duveen, you don't think the ballet is going to suffer a mortal blow by losing Ron?

SAM. I think the ballet will survive. *(To* RON*)* What are you going to do, then, Ron?

RON. I'm not quite sure. Rose knows a man who runs a travel agency who needs some dough and would take a partner. Only it's a ten to six job.

*(*SAM *smiles understandingly.)*

A more attractive idea is for Rose and me to get ourselves a small picture gallery in Paris.

SAM. I didn't know you liked pictures.

RON. I don't know that I do, but Rose does, and I'm learning fast. Aren't I, darling?

ROSE. *(fondly)* Frankly, no. Besides, I'm a terrible teacher. Still, a picture gallery would be fun. It'd probably be on the rocks after a month, but it'd be fun. *(She holds* **RON***'s hand.)*

HETTIE. *(getting up, suddenly)* I'm not speeding the parting guest, but you said something about Mr. Duveen having the Rolls to take him back, and I'd better warn Gaston.

ROSE. Yes, that's right.

*(**HETTIE** goes out)*

SAM. It's very kind.

ROSE. Not at all. Taxis down here are appallingly expensive.

RON. Did you sell the Thunderbird?

SAM. No. I've lent it until I get back from New York.

RON. *(casually)* To Michel?

SAM. Yes.

ROSE. Is it tonight you're going, Mr Duveen?

SAM. No, Mrs Bradford, tomorrow night – from Paris!

RON. Darling, why all this Mr Duveen, Mrs Bradford stuff? You've had a very nice lunch together – and I happen to know – because both of you have taken me aside separately and said it to me – that you each think the other's heaven—

ROSE. ⎫ *(murmuring* ⎧ Ron – really—
SAM. ⎭ *together)* ⎩ How embarrassing can you get?

RON. Well, you both said exactly the same thing to me. You both said she – or he – is far nicer than I expected. Anyone denying that?

(There is no answer.)

So why in hell can't you call each other Sam and Rose?

ROSE. *(after a pause)* We come from a politer generation than yours. We wait for permission before we Christian-name each other. *(Smiling)* Isn't that right, Sam?

SAM. *(smiling back)* It certainly is, Rose. Except that you shouldn't lie by including me in your generation.

(**HETTIE** *comes back with three letters which she hands to* **ROSE**.)

Or, if it comes to that, by excluding Ron's from yours.

ROSE. *(beginning to open the letters)* A woman is as old as she feels, isn't she? And I usually feel old enough to be his grandmother. Would you excuse me?

SAM. Of course.

(**ROSE** *reads two of the letters.*)

RON. What's the ballet you're doing in New York?

SAM. It's not New York. I'm going on to Hollywood.

RON. What film?

SAM. I don't know. I don't even know who's going to be in it.

RON. *(smiling)* But you know the money.

SAM. *(smiling back)* Just a vague idea.

RON. Good?

SAM. Best yet. That's still not good – but – better—

ROSE. *(to* **HETTIE**, *indicating letters)* That's a firm no. That's a qualified yes. *(Giving* **HETTIE** *the third letter unopened)* And that you can throw away.

HETTIE. Shouldn't you at least take a glance at the postmark?

ROSE. *(glancing at the envelope)* All right. So he's back. I knew he was about due.

(*She hands the letter back to* **HETTIE**, *making a gesture of tearing it up.* **KETTIE** *nods and goes out.*)

RON. Kurt?

ROSE. Yes.

SAM. Kurt Mast?

ROSE. That's right. My ex-intended.

SAM. *(nodding)* I read that interview he gave in Capri – the one where he said that there was no other man in your life but himself and that the marriage in Düsseldorf would take place precisely as planned. I thought that was rather sad.

ROSE. Why sad? It was just a silly lie. I haven't had any contact with Kurt for two months.

SAM. I'm sure.

RON. What's sad, then?

SAM. That he should find it necessary to his pride to tell such a silly lie. This is one story he couldn't buy off – and it was plainly the one that has hurt him the most. He must love you very much – that man.

(**FIONA,** *who has been reading the 'History of Western Philosophy' by Bertrand Russell, raises her head for just one quick glance at* **SAM.** *Apparently he has been the first of the adults to say something that has interested her.*)

RON. Who doesn't?

SAM. Who indeed?

ROSE. I don't think you need be too sorry for Kurt, Sam. He can look after himself. After all, he has the means.

SAM, They're a bit material, aren't they – in a crisis like this? Material enough to be immaterial, I'd have thought.

(Pause)

RON. I should have warned you about Sam, darling. He only really likes people he can feel sorry for, so he tries to find some reason to feel sorry for everyone in the world. Like me, for instance. When we first met he felt sorry for me because I could do six pirouettes dead on the spot and none of the others could. Isn't that true, Sam?

SAM. *(quietly)* Yes, Ron. That's completely true.

(**FIONA** *gets up.*)

FIONA. Mummy, may I go down to the pool?

ROSE. Isn't it a bit soon after lunch, dear?

FIONA. Oh, that's just an old person's – I mean an older person's superstition. *(Extending her hand)* Good-bye, Mr. Duveen.

SAM. Good-bye.

(**ROSE** *is looking at the recording machine, which is on a table.*)

ROSE. Have you been using this, this morning?

FIONA. *(casually)* No, Mummy.

ROSE. *(sharply)* Oh God, why do you lie? It's so idiotic. Who else uses this but you?

FIONA. *(sullenly)* I was going to use it and then I didn't.

ROSE. You did use it, but you don't want me to hear the result. That's it, isn't it?

(**FIONA** *does not reply.*)

All right. I'll respect the injunction. What play did you do?

FIONA. *The Seagull.*

ROSE. One day would you let me hear you reading a part? Any part?

FIONA. Yes, Mummy,

SAM. Is the young lady going to be an actress?

RON. She's mad about it. She's not half bad either. I've heard her.

ROSE. *(bitterly)* You're privileged.

RON. What do you think, Sam?

SAM. *(looking at* **FIONA** *appraisingly)* Can I ask you a question? An impertinent question?

FIONA. They're the ones I prefer.

SAM. Do you think acting's going to be fun?

FIONA. *(after a pause)* No. I think it's going to be hell.

SAM. *(nodding approvingly)* Good. You may make an actress.

FIONA. That's a trick question, *that* one. I know it. Still I answered it truthfully.

SAM. I'm sure you did. I can see you've inherited your mother's honesty. Good luck to you, anyway.

(FIONA *turns to the steps right to be stopped by* ROSE.)

ROSE. I want you to be ready to come out to dinner tonight, Fiona. I've promised to take you to the de Tocquevilles. Eight o'clock.

FIONA. (*quickly*) No, I can't. Not at eight. That's the time I'm going with Hettie to the station.

(*Pause*)

ROSE. You're doing what, Fiona?

FIONA. Hasn't she told you yet?

ROSE. (*bewildered*) No.

(*She looks round at* RON *who nods quietly.*)

(*To* RON) *You* knew?

RON. Yes.

ROSE. Where's she going to?

RON. (*shrugging*) Back to Scotland, I think.

(*Pause*)

ROSE. Why on earth hasn't she said something? Was she thinking of sneaking out of my life without saying a damn word?

(SAM *is looking at the view. Both he and* FIONA *are uncomfortable.*)

RON. I think the plot was to tell you only when all her bags were at the station and whatever you said to her couldn't make her change her mind.

ROSE. And that plot you encouraged?

RON. I didn't actually discourage it.

(ROSE *looks in bewilderment from* RON *to* FIONA. *Both look at her with differing degrees of sympathy.* SAM *is not looking at anyone.*)

ROSE. (*at length*) All right, Fiona. I won't take you to the de Tocquevilles. You can see Hettie off.

FIONA. Thank you, Mummy.

(She goes off to the pool. RON. turns to RON.)

ROSE. Ron. Oh, Ron. What is it?

(RON gets up from his chair and limps over to her, putting his arm around her. SAM is still staring at the view.)

RON. You know what it is.

ROSE. Damn her. Damn her. Damn her.

RON. It's best, you know.

ROSE. Without saying a word—

RON. *(sincerely)* I'm sorry. I'm awfully sorry, my darling. I knew how you'd feel. I told her what she was going to do to you.

ROSE. You could have got her to stay, couldn't you?

RON. By dying?

ROSE. *(fiercely)* Wasn't there anything you could say to her?

RON. Nothing. Nothing in the world. You know how she feels.

(He kisses her tenderly.)

ROSE. *(defiantly)* All right. Let her go. Let them all go. *(She turns to SAM.)* I'm so sorry. A little domestic crisis. Not really important.

(SAM bows politely and understandingly.)

Hettie – my housekeeper – is leaving – after five years – without thinking of even saying goodbye.

SAM. *(murmuring)* I'm sorry.

ROSE. I'm not. I agree with Ron. It's for the best. She was always damned inefficient, anyway. What about our lunch today? A pâté en croute, followed by a vol-au-vent. Does she want to suffocate us with pastry—

(HETTIE comes in. ROSE turns quickly away from her.)

HETTIE. The taxi's here for Ron.

(There is a pause. **ROSE**, *at length, nerves herself for the ordeal of turning and looking at* **HETTIE**.*)*

ROSE. *(quietly)* What was that, Hettie?

HETTIE. I said the taxi was here for Ron.

ROSE. Why a taxi?

HETTIE. *(patiently)* Because the Rolls is taking Mr Duveen to Monte, and Ron, as you know, can't drive his car, and I've far too much to do this afternoon to drive him to the hospital and wait for an hour for his treatment—

ROSE. Far too much to do? Yes. I suppose you have.

*(***HETTIE**, *at the tone of* **ROSE**'s *voice, turns to* **RON**, *who nods.)*

RON. Yes. She knows.

HETTIE. Good. Now I don't have to tell her.

ROSE. But you can tell me the time of your train.

HETTIE. Eight thirty-five – the Blue Train minor – the one that takes third-class compartments—

ROSE. *(coldly and politely)* Oh. Then at least I'll have a chance of seeing you for a moment before you go.

HETTIE. If you want to take it. *(She turns to go.)*

ROSE. Hettie.

*(***HETTIE** *turns back.)*

Is there any significance in the date?

HETTIE. August the tenth? Yes, of course. I don't like anniversaries but I always remember them.

ROSE. I don't remember them until I'm forced to.

HETTIE. Five years to the day makes things tidier, don't you think?

(She goes out. **RON** *hobbles over to* **ROSE**.*)*

RON. Don't be too angry with her. It's just blind jealousy – that's all. We can't any of us help our feelings, can we? *(He kisses her.)*

ROSE. No. We can't. *(To* **SAM***)* Oh dear. Wouldn't this be a nicer world if we could?

SAM. *(quoting* HETTIE*)* It might 'make things tidier'. Whether a tidier world would be a nicer world is a different matter.

RON. *(going up to him)* Well, goodbye, Sam. I'm glad you came up today. I'd have hated you to have gone off into the blue with – well – the way things were—

SAM. *(shaking hands)* The way things were wasn't so bad, you know, Ron.

RON. Well, I mean – considering— *(He pauses.)*

SAM. *(quietly)* Considering?

RON. *(shrugging, embarrassed)* Just considering. Anyway, I'm glad you've seen what I mean about Rose. *(Earnestly)* That was on the level, wasn't it – what you said to me about her just now?

SAM. *(to* ROSE, *with a smile)* Ron has all the suspiciousness of extreme immaturity. *(To* RON*)* Yes, Ron. What I said to you about Rose just now was entirely on the level.

RON. Good. Well, sorry I've got to dash off, but this masseur geezer's not one to be kept waiting.

SAM. *(suddenly, with eagerness)* The part to worry about, Ron, is this muscle here— *(he points to his own foot)* – because that's where you get your elevation. *(He remembers suddenly and stops. With a smile)* But of course a travel agent or a picture dealer doesn't have to worry about elevation, does he?

RON. *(smiling)* He doesn't have to worry about anything. Anything in the world. Well, goodbye, and good luck in Hollywood.

SAM. Same to you.

RON. Hope you *can* make the wedding, after all.

SAM. If I'm anywhere near Paris next month I certainly will.

RON. *(rather shyly)* Would it be any inducement if I said you could be best man?

SAM. To me it would. I doubt if it would to M.G.M. Still, let's hope I can make it.

(They shake hands, a shade of awkwardness on both sides. Then **RON** *turns to* **ROSE.**)

RON. *(kissing her)* I'll go to the beach after the treatment. Can you come?

ROSE. No. Not allowed it.

RON. I'd forgotten. Meet you at the de Tocquevilles then.

ROSE. All right.

(He embraces her with sudden warmth.)

RON. I don't care what anybody says. It's just a bloody miracle – and that's a fact.

ROSE. *(laughing)* Can a miracle be a fact?

RON. This one can.

(He releases her and hobbles to the door, which **SAM** *holds open for him. He looks at* **SAM** *as if wanting to say something, checks himself and contents himself with a nervous smile and a pat on the arm. He goes out.* **ROSE** *wanders to the side of the terrace left, to watch him go. She waves and blows a kiss. We hear the sound of the taxi starting.)*

ROSE. *(musingly)* Do you think a miracle can be a fact?

SAM. *(quietly)* No.

*(***ROSE,** *waving goodbye to* **RON,** *turns suddenly and looks at* **SAM.**)*

ROSE. I love him more than life, you know.

SAM. More than whose life? Yours or his?

(Pause. **ROSE** *offers* **SAM** *a cigarette. He shakes his head. She takes one herself.)*

ROSE. Just a woman's sentimental exaggeration. I'm sorry. I only meant that I love him very much.

SAM. *(politely lighting her cigarette)* Yes.

ROSE. *(defiantly)* And will for life.

*(***SAM** *does not reply.)*

Why don't you say yes to that?

SAM. I told you that I don't believe in miracles.

(Pause)

ROSE. (sadly) Are you an enemy, after all?

SAM. For an honest and intelligent woman you ask some very unsubtle questions.

ROSE. For an honest and intelligent man you give some very indirect answers. Are you an enemy?

SAM. How can I answer that one except indirectly? I'm a friend of his, and I like and admire you.

ROSE. But?

SAM. (with a sigh) But I'm an enemy.

ROSE. Why?

SAM. (gently) Wouldn't it be easier for you to answer that yourself? You only need one convenient word.

ROSE. I know. It's too convenient. Ron used it about Hettie and it isn't true of her. I don't think it's true of you either. Why are you an enemy? Because I'm taking him away from the ballet?

SAM. Of course.

ROSE. (smiling) You said the ballet would survive without Ron.

SAM. I didn't say Ron would survive without the ballet.

ROSE. (smiling) He told me you'd a one-track mind. Ron doesn't even like the ballet. It's not important to him. at all.

SAM. He doesn't think it is. It's too much like work, and when there's a rich lady around—

ROSE. Not so damn rich. After selling this house and the pictures we'll only have about three and a half thousand a year—

SAM. And you to look after him.

ROSE. Yes.

SAM. The combination will be quite enough, I'd say. Travel Agency. Picture Gallery. What a hope. He won't last a week in either. I can see you don't know your Ron as well as I thought.

ROSE. Why is the ballet so important to him?

SAM. Because it's a job he does quite well, and the only one he ever will do, which I believe you really know just as well as I. Anyway, it's the one job he had the guts to teach himself to do when he was a kid. Fighting his father to do it, too – which was good for that thing we laughingly call his soul. Oh yes. He doesn't know it, of course – Ron doesn't know anything about himself – but the ballet's as important to him as – well – as a lifebelt is to a non-swimmer in a rough sea.

ROSE. *(thoughtfully)* He *could* go on with the ballet – I suppose.

(SAM laughs shortly.)

(Rather angrily) I could persuade him to, I'm sure.

SAM. *(quietly)* Could you persuade him to class by nine in the morning? Could you persuade him off the vin rosé and the night clubs and the weekends in Rome and the yachts and the late-night parties?

ROSE. Yes. I think I could.

SAM. I called you honest a moment ago.

ROSE. Well, I could try.

SAM. If you did it would only lead to a series of bloody rows, and an even earlier bust-up than will happen anyway. No. Take him off to Paris and the travel agency and/or picture gallery. That's much better – for both of you. I must *go*.

ROSE. *(stopping him)* You seem damn sure this won't last.

SAM. Yes. I am.

ROSE. Why?

SAM. I know my Ron.

ROSE. You don't know me.

SAM. Only what I've read in the Sunday papers and seen today. A lady who's got exactly where she wants by marrying four husbands she didn't love, and now thinks it's time to settle down happily and marry a fifth that she does.

ROSE. At least you grant that.

SAM. I've already said so. It's the duration I don't.

ROSE. How long do you give it?

SAM. The record for loving Ron up to now is, I believe, six months.

ROSE. I won't have much trouble breaking that record.

SAM. No. You're fairly tough, I'd say. You might even double it.

ROSE. Oh, for heaven's sake. I said a lifetime.

SAM. Don't worry. It'll seem a lifetime.

ROSE. What's so damn hard about loving Ron?

SAM. What's hard about loving anyone who can't love back?

ROSE. He can love back. He loves me.

(SAM *says nothing.*)

Anyway he needs me.

SAM. Oh yes. He's always needed people and always will.

ROSE. Fine. That's all I want. Why should I want more?

SAM. *(slowly)* Why indeed? But I see you're rather new to this business of being needed by Ron. You don't seem to understand that the Rons of this world always end by hating the people they need. They can't help it. It's compulsive. Of course it probably isn't plain hate. It's love-hate, or hate-love, or some other Freudian jargon – but it's still a pretty good imitation of the real thing. You see – when day after day, night after night – you're being kicked hard and steadily in the teeth, it's not all that important what the character who's doing it feels for you. You can leave that to the psychiatrists to work out. All you can do is to nurse a broken jaw and, in your own good time, get the hell out. I'll give you six months – from the honeymoon. Take a bet?

ROSE. No. I don't want your money.

SAM. Why not? It's as hard-earned as yours.

ROSE. *(at length with anger)* You seem to think you know an awful lot about Ron – after only six months.

SAM. Six months? Who said—

ROSE. *(quickly)* I'm sorry. I thought—

SAM. *(equally quickly)* Did you? That's interesting. Oh no. I've taken my kicks in the teeth for longer than six months. In fact for – let's think now – pretty near seven years. But that's all right, you see. The kicks have been only intermittent – with intervals for recovery. I don't see him all that often. And anyway I've learnt to wear a gum-shield.

(Pause)

ROSE. I don't think I've got you straight, Sam. What's your interest in Ron?

SAM. Father figure.

ROSE. Can you enlarge?

SAM. I met him when he was at the Ballet Rambert in '52. He'd run away from home to join it. His mother was dead, and he hated his father. He wasn't liked by the other kids and in London he lived alone. You feel he needs looking after now, and you're right, but you can imagine how much he needed it then. Well – I provided that need – and have provided it – in the background – off and on – more or less until you came along. I got him this job here – and in spite of commitments, I've usually managed to be around when he's needed me.

ROSE. I see.

(Pause)

SAM. *(slowly)* There are ways and ways of saying 'I see'. You've chosen that way. Who gave you that idea? Ron, I suppose—

ROSE. I don't know. I can't remember. No, I don't think so.

SAM. I bet he did.

ROSE. Perhaps he did. Perhaps he was right to.

SAM. *(quietly)* He did, and he wasn't right to. Would you try to get this into your Wolfenden-conscious mind? Feelings can't sometimes be helped, but the expression of them can. They can and they are.

ROSE. That sounds very noble.

SAM. No. Not noble. Difficult and rather humiliating – and well – just generally pretty good hell. But not ignoble.

ROSE. I'm sorry.

SAM. That's all right.

ROSE. I'm sorry you quarrelled.

SAM. So am I.

ROSE. Still, you've made it up now.

SAM. Yes. We'll nod to each other in the Ritz bar.

ROSE. No more than that?

SAM. No.

ROSE. Why not?

SAM. I've had a belly-full. Seven years is a long time. Besides – there's someone else now.

ROSE. Yes, I'd heard. Pity.

SAM. Not a pity at all.

ROSE. Was it all because of me?

SAM. Is that what he told you?

ROSE. More or less.

SAM. Rather more than less, I imagine. *(Imitating)* 'Sam's so jealous and possessive, Rose – I can't tell you. Ever since you came into my life he's been like a fiend – and I can't stand it—' Something like that?

ROSE. Something. It was about your being jealous of the new car – because it showed up yours—

(SAM laughs with genuine and affectionate amusement.)

SAM. Oh good. Very good. Real vintage Ron. Jealous of the car. Poor little bastard. *(Quietly, facing her.)* I came over this year to do three ballets. Ron was to have had the lead in all of them. No favouritism. He *is* their best virtuoso dancer. He did two – could have been better, but all right – and then we were rehearsing the third when you came into his life. After he'd cut two rehearsals I fired him, and got another boy – not too good, but coming along. At least he works. When Ron heard the news he did his best to carve up the new boy, then came home and staged a phoney suicide scene with me, and when that didn't work got into his car and roared off into the night. Up here, to you, I suppose. I didn't follow as I used to, because I'd had it. Had it for keeps. That's the story. Not exciting, but – conclusive. *(He looks over the side of the terrace.)* I see the car's waiting. I'd really better be going.

ROSE. *(absently)* So soon?

SAM. I've got a lot of packing—

ROSE. *(a shade hysterically)* Everybody's packing.

SAM. *(extending his hand)* Well – thank you for a very delightful lunch—

ROSE. *(taking his hand)* If you've had it – why are you an enemy?

(SAM smiles.)

SAM. As we used to say once in Bomber Command – bang on. Because, I suppose, I haven't really had it. I don't want ever to see him again – that's true – but I still hate the thought of seven years' work – God, what work – utterly wasted – thrown into the ashcan – no return – no return at all. I'm not talking about the ballet, you know. He'd never have been a Nijinsky. He might have made Covent Garden in minor leads in a year or two – but he wasn't ever going to have biographies written about him – even if he'd really worked, which, even without you, wasn't very likely. No. It's him. It's the human being I worked on – and tried to make a man of— *(He stops.)* Yes. That's an easy laugh, isn't it? Still, it's true— Anyway, it's stupid to care. What does one Ron Vale matter in this world, more or less?

(Pause)

ROSE. *(hotly)* You damn fool. Do you think I'd ever let him down?

SAM. Oh no, I don't. I'm sure, after you leave him, he'll have no reason to complain about the size of his allowance. At least he'll have no reason to – but if I know Ron – he will. Still, all your friends and the Press and your sixth husband will all say you've behaved very generously – considering. Of course he won't be able to go back to the ballet, because at his age you can't give it up even for six months. Besides, he'll have gone to seed a bit by then, probably off the rosé and on to the brandy, I should think. Still, in whatever queer bar he finds himself in London or Paris or New York, I'm sure he'll always be pointed out with some envy as Rose Fish's fifth – 'lucky guy. Doesn't have to work. He was a dancer, once, they say. Hard to believe now, looking at him. Let's go over and talk to him. He's fun when he's drunk.'

ROSE. *(laughing)* Do you think you can frighten me with a temperance play?

SAM. I know I can't frighten you at all. How could I? What have *you* got to be frightened of?

ROSE. *(after a pause)* Well – walking into that bar and seeing him, perhaps.

SAM. No risk. You wouldn't go to that sort of bar.

ROSE. That's funny – from you.

SAM. I know, but I wouldn't either.

ROSE. You think – you really think – I shouldn't go ahead?

SAM. It doesn't matter a damn what I think. You'll go ahead anyway. You've earned your right to your bit of fun, and nothing and nobody in the world is going to stop you having it. Even if it is fun with another human being's life—

ROSE. As Ron would say – a pure case of F.U., Jack, I'm all right.

SAM. Yes. As Ron would say. Well— *(He turns.)*

ROSE. *(quietly, stopping him)* I just want to correct a misconception, that's all. The word 'fun'. I'm going ahead with Ron – but it's not for my fun. It's because his needing me is – well – the best thing that's ever happened to me, and without it I wouldn't see much point in going on living. That's not a woman's exaggeration, Sam. It's the simple truth. I can't explain why it means so much. Hettie quoted Horace at my head the other day. Something about expelling Nature with a pitchfork, but it always comes back. Meaning, I suppose, that since Birmingham I've suppressed my natural instincts, and now Nature has taken a mean revenge—

SAM. Oh no. Hettie's wrong on that. What you feel for Ron isn't Nature's revenge on you. It's much more your revenge on Nature.

ROSE. *(very angry)* That *sounds* good. Does it *mean* anything?

SAM. Yes, I'd say it does. I'd say it means that just because you've had a real tough time fighting Nature to get where you are, now you're going to turn the tables on the old bag by taking a boy nine years younger than you and turning him from a fairly good virtuoso dancer into a male Rose Fish.

(Pause)

ROSE. *(in a whisper)* You're brutal.

SAM. I'm not. The truth is.

ROSE. *(raising her voice)* It isn't the truth. Remember what he was like when I met him.

SAM. *(quietly)* I do. Very well.

ROSE. That side was always in him.

SAM. I know. It just needed bringing out.

ROSE. If it hadn't been me, it'd have been someone else.

SAM. Quite likely. It just happened to be you.

(Pause)

ROSE. God, I hate you.

SAM. Pity, because I don't hate you. In fact I like you very much.

(Pause)

ROSE. *(pitifully)* Oh God – Sam – please – you don't understand—

*(*HETTIE *comes in.)*

HETTIE. *(ignoring* ROSE, *to* SAM*)* The chauffeur asked me to tell you that the car is waiting to take you to Monte Carlo.

SAM. Yes, I know. I'm sorry to have kept him.

HETTIE. Oh, that's all right. He's used to waiting.

(She begins to gather a few personal oddments from the terrace.)

SAM. *(formally to* ROSE*)* Well – thank you once again for a delightful lunch.

ROSE. *(in the same tone)* Not at all, I'm so glad you could come.

SAM. *(stopping her as she moves towards the stairs)* No, please don't see me off. Those stairs tire you. I saw that this morning.

ROSE. *(smiling)* They do a bit. It's this blasted cough of mine. I hope to see you at the wedding, after all.

SAM. Yes. I'll make it, if I can, I promise you. Goodbye.

ROSE. Goodbye.

*(*SAM *goes out.* HETTIE *is still gathering things.)*

HETTIE. *(her back to* ROSE*)* Is *Napoleon's Loves* mine or yours?

ROSE. Yours.

HETTIE. And *Over the Seas to Skye?*

ROSE. Mine.

HETTIE. Yes, of course.

ROSE. Hettie, why are you leaving me?

HETTIE. God, you should know that by now.

ROSE. In a nutshell – once more.

(She sits down in a chair, not looking at **HETTIE**, *who now turns and stares at her.)*

HETTIE. Because I hate dishonesty and I hate funk.

ROSE. Funk? You haven't said that before.

HETTIE. Trying to have your cake and eat it *is* a form of funk. You made your bed a long time ago—

ROSE. Don't mix your metaphors.

HETTIE. I certainly will. I'll give you a third if you like. Time off for 'Love in a Cottage' was never a clause in your original contract – and it's just plain cheating for you to pretend it was. Well, I hate cheating, I hate dishonesty and I hate funk. At least – from you.

*(***ROSE*** makes no reply.)*

(At length) All right?

ROSE. *(quietly, without looking at her)* All right.

*(***HETTIE*** goes out. ***ROSE*** sits quite motionless, staring ahead of her. ***FIONA*** comes on from the steps right. Her dishevelled hair shows she has been swimming. Seeing her mother she stops resignedly, preparing to be spoken to. But ***ROSE*** is utterly oblivious of her. ***FIONA*** looks at her curiously, shrugs her shoulders and goes into the house. ***ROSE*** continues to stare into space.)*

*(The lights fade and when they come on again the sun has set and there is very little light on the terrace. ***ROSE*** has not changed her attitude.)*

*(***HETTIE*** comes on from the house. She is dressed for her journey.)*

HETTIE. You ought to be changing for your dinner party.

ROSE. *(not changing her attitude)* What's the time?

HETTIE. After seven. *(She turns back towards the house.)*

ROSE. Don't go. *(She gets up and goes to the drink tray.)* We'd better at least have a last drink together.

HETTIE. Thanks. I'll have a beer.

ROSE. *(wearily)* If you'd been me, Hettie, these last few weeks – how would you have coped with it all?

HETTIE. Oh, I'd have told him to buzz off.

ROSE. If you'd really been me you might not have found that very easy.

HETTIE. No. Damn difficult, I should think. But that's what I'd have done.

ROSE. Supposing he'd refused to buzz off?

HETTIE. Then I'd have buzzed off myself.

ROSE. Supposing he'd have followed?

HETTIE. You're putting his feeling for you a bit high there, aren't you?

ROSE. *(quietly)* No. Not at the moment. He needs me with him.

HETTIE. Well, then I'd just have told him that I didn't need *him* with *me*.

ROSE. Do you think he'd have believed that? You've seen the way I behave when he's anywhere near me—

HETTIE. Yes. Like an idiotic schoolgirl. Well, then – last, but best – I'd just have seen to it that he didn't need me any more, I'd have destroyed this damn need of his—

ROSE. How?

HETTIE. *(shrugging)* Give me time. I haven't thought. *(After a moment)* Well, I imagine what he needs from you is security, protection, permanence – the usual mother business. That right?

ROSE. Yes.

HETTIE. Well, then I'd have done something so brutal and outrageous to him, that I'd have blown all that security stuff up for him right in his face. There wouldn't have been a shred of sonny-boy's mummy-need left.

ROSE. *(nodding slowly)* You haven't thought, you said. Give me time, you said. And yet after a few seconds you arrive at exactly the same solution that I've taken the whole damn afternoon to find. You must think an awful lot faster than me, Hettie. But then you're not involved, are you, and emotions, they do say, muddle the brain—

(Her voice, relaxed before, is now tense and strained. She turns to the recording machine, left on a table, where **FIONA** *must have used it.)*

Show me how this thing works, would you? I've forgotten.

*(***HETTIE***, staring at* ***ROSE***, puzzled, walks across to the machine, and switches it on. A red light begins to glow.)*

HETTIE. Do you want to record or listen?

ROSE. Record.

*(***HETTIE*** switches a knob.)*

HETTIE. *(pointing)* There's the microphone there. You don't have to talk right into it. Just stand about where you are – that should be all right. It's not going on tape yet, but it's live. Just say something, so I can adjust the volume.

ROSE. Hullo, Ron. Hullo, Ron. Hullo, Ron.

*(***HETTIE*** adjusts the volume control.)*

HETTIE. That's about right. Now when you let that button up you're recording. If anything goes wrong, or you can't think what you want to say, press that button down and it stops the tape.

ROSE. I see.

HETTIE. It's quite simple. *(She moves to the door.)*

ROSE. Hettie.

*(***HETTIE*** turns.)*

Stay, will you?

HETTIE. All right.

ROSE. *You'd* better work that button. It *is* just possible that something might go wrong – or I mightn't be able to think what to say.

(Her voice is beginning to show that overwhelming emotion is not far away.)

(To **HETTIE***)* On.

*(***HETTIE** *presses the button. The reel of tape begins slowly to revolve.)*

Ron, my dear, I'm sorry to have to use this machine to talk to you, but I'm bad at writing letters, as you know, and I thought anyway you might prefer to hear what I've got to say to you in my own voice. I should have said it to you personally I suppose, but quite frankly, I funked it. I've got to try and tell you why I've decided to leave you and go back to Kurt—

(She makes a quick sign to **HETTIE** *to stop the tape. Until now her voice has been hard and casual, but she has felt the tears coming. She takes a sip of her drink, then nods to* **HETTIE***, who switches the tape on.)*

I'm afraid it'll be a big shock for you, darling, when you hear it, and I'm sorry—

(Her voice is again unemotional.)

I've hated doing it, too, because you know how I've felt about you – that's to say until just lately, when I admit I've had to do a tiny bit of acting – because I did fix up things with Kurt when he got back a few days ago. But you mustn't think that my feelings for you haven't been quite sincere – anyway in the beginning. I did love you, you know, Ron. I really did—

(She makes a sign to **HETTIE** *and breaks down completely.* **HETTIE** *watches her from the machine.)*

HETTIE. I shouldn't go on with this, if I were you. Why not a letter?

ROSE. With tear-stains all over it – shaking handwriting? No, this is the way. This is the way all right. Just give me a moment. I've got to finish it now – this minute, otherwise there isn't a hope.

(She dries her eyes. **HETTIE** *goes back to the machine.)*

(Murmuring) I did love you, Ron. I really did.

(She nods to **HETTIE** *who switches it on.)*

But my trouble has always been that I can't love anyone for very long. And anyway it wouldn't have worked. It really wouldn't. Darling – you know me. Could you really have seen *me* living on in a three-room flat? *Me,* after all I've done to escape from just that sort of life? And, anyway, what girl in her senses would turn down fifty million? Well, that's all, darling. You won't see me again. Not ever. I'm going off somewhere with Kurt for a week or so. After a bit I don't suppose you'll mind. You'd better go back to the ballet, when your ankle's all right again. After all, it's still money, isn't it? Goodbye, darling. Goodbye, and I suppose I should say – thanks, too—

*(***HETTIE*** switches it off, as* **ROSE** *turns away in tears once more.)*

*(***HETTIE*** goes up to her, and puts her arm round her shoulders.)*

ROSE. Why couldn't you have left me in peace?

HETTIE. I'm sorry. Oh God, I'm sorry.

ROSE. You don't need to go now.

HETTIE. *(pointing to recording machine)* We can wipe it out. I could be wrong, you know. I'm pretty old. Perhaps I don't know about things the way I think I do.

ROSE. *(still in tears)* Ron says it's just jealousy—

HETTIE. *(quietly)* It might be only that. Shall we wipe it out? It's very easy—

ROSE. No. *(She recovers herself a little.)* I'm sorry, Hettie, it's just that I've got to blame somebody. It wasn't you, anyway. I'd made up my own mind an hour ago, *(Wiping her eyes)* I think you *do* know about things. I wish to God you didn't, but you do. Now listen. I'm going out now.

HETTIE. To Kurt?

ROSE. God, no. Not tonight, anyway. Not for an awful lot of nights, if at all. Anyway, I don't know if he'll have me. Did you read that letter?

HETTIE. Yes.

ROSE. Is it—

(HETTIE *nods.*)

I'm not going to think about that now. I'll go to an hotel tonight.

HETTIE. Do you want me to come with you?

ROSE. No. You'd better stay here. Ron will be calling from the de Tocquevilles when he finds I'm not there. You'd better tell him to come straight home, as there's an important message here from me. Don't be with him when he hears it.

(HETTIE *shakes her head.*)

And Hettie – I know what you feel about him, but he's going to be more unhappy tonight and for a few days to come than he's ever been in his life before. Perhaps than he ever will be. Be kind.

(HETTIE *nods.*)

It won't be too easy. He's bound to be pretty bloody – particularly about me. Just remember – the bloodier the better. It might be an idea to get his friend Sam round. He'll need someone pretty close to look after him tonight – say the right things and lend a shoulder to cry on—

(HETTIE *nods again.* ROSE *is on the point of tears once more.*)

Oh, Hettie. (*She stops.*)

HETTIE. Yes?

ROSE. (*trying to smile*) I was just thinking – if only it could have been me—

(*She goes out quickly.*)

(*Curtain*)

Scene Two

(Scene: The same, three months later.)

(It is about eight in the evening. A large cocktail party has only just finished, and the terrace shows signs of it. Through the sitting-room window we can see white-coated servants clearing up. On the terrace a card table has been laid out, and at it **KURT** *is playing a game of baccarat with* **HETTIE** *and* **MONA**. *He is taking the bank and has just finished a hand.)*

KURT. Faites vos jeux, Mesdames et Mesdemoiselles. Faites vos jeux—

MONA. Well, this time he must lose.

(She takes a five-thousand-franc note from her bag and puts it in front of her.)

KURT. Five thousand francs premier tableau and—

(He turns to **HETTIE**.*)*

HETTIE. Ten.

KURT. Ten francs deuxieme tableau.

*(**HETTIE** puts a coin down, **KURT** deals the cards – one to each, one to himself, then another to each, another for himself. **MONA**, on his right, looks at her cards.)*

MONA. Card.

HETTIE. *(looking at hers)* No.

*(**KURT** turns his cards on the table.)*

KURT. *(gurgling delightedly)* Et neuf en banque.

(He takes the money from both sides.)

MONA. Hell. How do you do it? Stack the cards?

KURT. Of course. Before the party I am spending hours making up this shoe.

MONA. I wouldn't be surprised.

HETTIE. Well, that cleans me. *(She gets up.)*

KURT. Go on, Hettie. Your credit is good.

HETTIE. Listen – my credit is terrible. Ask the Sporting Club.

MONA. Do you still owe them, Hettie?

HETTIE. Seven fifty thousand.

MONA. But that's nothing. You *did* owe them a fortune once, didn't you?

HETTIE. Yes, once. In the days when they thought an English lady of tide couldn't be a crook.

MONA. How much?

HETTIE. Ten million.

MONA. And you've managed to pay all that back?

HETTIE. Over the years – in dribs and drabs.

MONA. Why didn't you ever ask Rose to settle it for you?

HETTIE. Because that's exactly what she would have done. *(Meaningly)* Of course if someone else had offered—

KURT. A measly two hundred and twenty thousand is all I am winning tonight. Still, it is paying for the party—

(**KURT**, *puffing contentedly at his cigar, is engaged in counting a pile of notes,* **HETTIE,** *behind* **KURT,** *makes a gesture at his head, indicating to* **MONA** *exactly whom she means by someone else.*)

MONA. Why don't you pay it, Kurt?

KURT. Pay what?

MONA. What Hettie still owes the Sporting Club.

KURT. How much is that?

MONA. *(making it sound small)* Seven fifty thousand.

(**KURT** *laughs politely – as at a joke.* **HETTIE** *shrugs resignedly.* **MONA** *smiles.*)

Well, it's been a lovely party, but I wish like hell I'd have gone when everyone else did. It might have saved me quite a bit of dough—

KURT. A few more hands. You will be winning. I guarantee.

MONA. O.K.

HETTIE. Aren't you cold out here?

MONA. No. It's still quite warm. *(As* **KURT** *deals)* My God, you were lucky with the weather this evening. If you'd had the real November stuff, we'd all have been sardines in there – hell, I haven't put any money up. I'm doubling up. Ten mille. O.K.

*(**KURT** nods.)*

How many people, Hettie? *(To* **KURT***)* Card.

HETTIE. Three hundred plus—

*(**FIONA** comes in, as **KURT** turns his own cards face upwards and grins.)*

MONA. Goddam you, Kurt, for a— *(Seeing* **FIONA***)* Oh hullo, Fiona.

FIONA. Hullo. *(To* **HETTIE***)* Where's Mummy?

HETTIE. Up in her room. She's not feeling well.

FIONA. Oh. I'm sorry.

*(**KURT** has given **MONA** a card and now turns his.)*

KURT. Neuf en banque. On paie partout.

MONA. Only your presence, Fiona, prevents me saying something that's in my mind. All right. Same again.

HETTIE. *(to* **FIONA***.)* Do you want her for anything special?

FIONA. She won't mind if I go before dinner instead of after, will she?

HETTIE. You know damn well she will. You know equally well she won't stop you.

FIONA. *(a shade unhappily for once)* They've planned something for me at the Ciel et Enfer. A sort of good-bye do.

MONA. *(laying down her new hand)* Eight. That's better.

*(**KURT** pays her.)*

All right. *(Pointing to her wager)* That stays.

FIONA. *(continuing)* I can't get out of it, Hettie. Really I can't.

HETTIE. *(sadly, after a pause)* I think you're being a bit of a rat, Fiona. It could be that this damn coast affects even children.

FIONA. *(rather near tears)* If Mummy wants to come to the airport to see me off, she can. I've always said she could, if she wanted to.

HETTIE. Yes, and I know the tone of voice you said it in. Anyway, do you suppose she wants to come to the airport surrounded by a mob of juvenile delinquents on Vespas? You're off to London, and she won't see you till the wedding – and a last meal with her wouldn't have been all that difficult to arrange, I'd have thought—

FIONA. *(her voice rising)* I couldn't help it, Hettie. I couldn't—

KURT. *(with a shout of triumph)* Neuf.

MONA. *(simultaneously)* Oh, my God! Not again.

FIONA. *(going to KURT to escape HETTIE.)* Are you winning?

KURT. *(throwing his arm round her waist)* Oh, my little Fiona. Yes, I am winning a little chicken food. *(He looks up at her.)* Do you know one day you are going to be a very beautiful heart-breaker. Yes, one day, I shall be being very proud of my little stepdaughter of the future.

FIONA. I don't want to break any hearts.

KURT. *(dealing another hand)* No?

FIONA. I just want mine broken – by the right person.

KURT. Very unbusinesslike. *(To MONA)* No cards? *(He turns his cards up.)* Egalité. *(To FIONA)* What time is your plane?

FIONA. Midnight, *(looking at HETTIE)* but I'm leaving the house before dinner.

KURT. Ah. Then I must be saying good-bye. *(He gets up.)*

FIONA. I'm not going just yet.

KURT. Ah, but I have three angry Swiss bankers waiting for me up at my house – and I have to see them before dinner.

FIONA. Why are they angry?

KURT. Because they are Swiss, because they are bankers, and because they are waiting. No bankers are used to waiting, even for me. *(Kissing her)* Good-bye, mein liebchen. Will you like your new stepfather?

FIONA. *(with patent insincerity)* Yes. Very much, I'm sure.

HETTIE. And she speaks from a wide experience of stepfathers, remember.

FIONA. *(ignoring her)* Mummy's not really ill, is she?

KURT. Oh no, no. A little tiredness – no more.

FIONA. *(looking firmly at* HETTIE*)* Good. I'll go and see her now. I've got something to ask her.

(She goes out.)

KURT. Three more hands, Mona?

MONA. O.K.

(He deals.)

It really was only tiredness, wasn't it? No card.

KURT. Sure, sure. *(He gives her a card and then another to himself.)* Goddam baccarat! Yes. Only tiredness – after the party—

HETTIE. *(with weary irony)* You know how people often get a bit tired after a party, Mona, and cough up blood. Nothing to worry about at all—

KURT. *(banging his cards angrily on the table)* You will please not be saying such things.

HETTIE. Why won't I?

MONA. Was it so bad?

KURT. Of course it wasn't so bad. Don't listen to this crazy woman. She will be making a drama of everything—

HETTIE. I haven't made much of a drama yet, have I? I haven't said that you're damn lucky it was such a slight attack and that your show-off party this afternoon might quite easily have bumped off your bride-to-be altogether.

KURT. Lady Henrietta – I must be asking you please to remember that in this house you are only a paid employee—

HETTIE. Not by you. I'm paid by a lady who has just been told by her doctors that if she doesn't have complete rest for three months in a sanatorium she'll be dead inside that time. I'm paid to look after that lady – as best I can – and I think in that capacity I've the right to make the comment that a party for over three hundred bods given in her own house, with herself as hostess and having to cope, wasn't the wisest way of following doctors' orders.

KURT. Go away. You are boring me. Mona – another hand.

(He deals the cards.)

(Explosively) Goddam, Hettie, it was she was wanting this party—

HETTIE. Of course it was. When she's in the sanatorium it'll be she who'll be wanting to give the parties there too. It's just that it might have been an idea to discourage her—

MONA. Card. There *were* rather a lot of people, Kurt—

KURT. *(angrily)* For a farewell to the Chateau Auguste one should be having tea and buns for six? *(Taking a card)* *One* against baccarat. Mine.

MONA. You're a wizard. Oh hell. Will your bankers still wait?

KURT. Sure they'll wait.

MONA. All right, then. One last hand.

(RON has walked quietly on to the terrace from the drive below. There has been no sound of a car arriving and both KURT and MONA are unaware of his presence. HETTIE sees him first.)

RON. *(nodding to her pleasantly)* Hullo, Hettie.

HETTIE. What are you doing here?

RON. I've come by invitation.

HETTIE. Whose invitation?

RON. Mona's. I'm the 'and friend' on her invitation card. Isn't that right, Mona? Hullo, Kurt.

KURT. *(with quiet anger, to* **MONA***)* This is true?

MONA. Of course not. As if I would—

KURT. *(to* **RON***)* You will please be leaving here at once – or do you want I shall be calling the police?

RON. Why the police? What's the fuss? I saw Mona in the casino last night, and she asked me to come with her to this party. If you doubt it – *(he produces a card from his pocket)* how is it I've got her invitation card?

MONA. It was a joke, Kurt. I'd had one too many, I never thought for a moment he'd take me seriously—

RON. But I did take you seriously, Mona. Very seriously. I heard this was going to be one of the best parties ever, and I particularly wanted to come.

HETTIE. Then why arrive after it's over?

RON. A good question, Hettie. I remember – you always ask good questions. Because I had a sudden rehearsal, and because I thought that the party – a party as grand and as lavish as this one – would probably go on after nine.

HETTIE. Well, it hasn't. So I don't see there's any particular reason for your staying around, do you?

RON. No. To be quite frank, I don't.

MONA. *(very hastily)* I'm leaving anyway, Ron.

RON. Good. You can give me a lift back into Cannes.

HETTIE. How did you get up here?

RON. By bus to the top of the road and walked from there.

KURT. *(laughing)* By bus?

RON. Yes. They have them you know, even on this coast.

KURT. And what has happened to the beautiful Lagonda? Sold?

RON. No. Not sold. *(He glances through the windows into the sitting-room.)*

HETTIE. No. She's not in there, Ron.

RON. I know she's not. She's in her bedroom. I saw the light coming up. *(To* MONA*)* Do you mind waiting just a second, darling, while I spend a penny?

(To HETTIE, *who has made an involuntary move to stop him going into the house.)*

It's all right, Hettie. I know the way.

*(*HETTIE *still bars the way.)*

I won't go upstairs. If you want to check on it, you can stand here and watch the staircase.

HETTIE. I will.

*(*RON *smiles and goes inside.* HETTIE *stations herself where she can see into the house.)*

MONA. *(to* KURT*)* Oh my God, Kurt – will you ever forgive me? But it wasn't my fault – it really wasn't. How could I know he was even remotely serious?

KURT. You gave him your card.

MONA. He took it. I showed it to him and he took it. At the bar, it was, in the Casino Municipale. That's where his company are dancing this week. *(Angrily)* Don't think it's a plot, for God's sake. I haven't seen the guy since Rose fired him – I swear it – not until last night when I was playing chemmy and—

KURT. *(to* HETTIE*)* What about his Lagonda?

HETTIE. *(gazing into the house)* He gave it back.

KURT. That is a damned lie. I would be knowing if he had given it back. It is not here, in the garage.

HETTIE. She wouldn't take it.

KURT. Where is it, then?

HETTIE. In no-man's-land. A garage in Juan. I have the keys and the registration book. No one is paying the garage, yet – but I pay for the petrol when I use it.

KURT. You use the car?

HETTIE. Oh yes.

(She turns from the window, satisfied **RON** *is on his way back.)*

Well, it seems silly just to let it sit there and rust, doesn't it?

*(***RON*** *comes back.)*

RON. *(looking at the table)* Who's been winning?

MONA. Kurt. He cleaned me. Come on, Ron.

RON. Would you like a hand, Kurt?

MONA. Don't be silly, Ron. Gome on.

RON. *(repeating steadily)* Would you like a hand, Kurt?

KURT. Sure. We'll play for your bus fare.

RON. Oh no. *(He throws down some notes.)* Not what you're used to playing for, I know, but a bit more than my bus fare. There's twenty-five thousand there.

KURT. *(with a smile)* You are being lucky in love again?

RON. No. Not in the way you mean. That's my week's salary – with extra for dancing the blue bird or Peter Pansy as you called it once – remember. I'll take the bank. *(He deals the cards.)*

KURT. Card.

*(***RON*** *turns his cards up. It is evidently an eight or nine. He shows no emotion, staring quietly at* ***KURT***. ***KURT*** *takes some notes from his pocket and throws them on the table.)*

Suivi.

*(***RON*** *deals the cards again.)*

No.

*(***RON*** *turns his cards up, and takes a card. Again he has won, but again his face shows no expression.* ***KURT*** *throws fifty thousand francs on to the table and turns to go.)*

RON. *(quietly)* Quitting, Kurt?

(KURT turns back and goes to the table. He raps his fingers on it in the gesture which means banco. RON deals.)

KURT. Card.

(RON gives him one, and then raps his own cards in the gesture which means that he is standing. KURT once more pulls out money and throws the notes on to the table.)

Suivi.

MONA. *(to RON)* For heaven's sake stop now, Ron. Take it in, and let's go, You've got nearly two hundred pounds—

RON. Yes, but if I give it again, I'd have nearly four hundred, wouldn't I?

MONA. Or nothing. More likely nothing.

HETTIE. Mona's right. You should take your money and think yourself damn lucky—

RON. *(gently)* But Kurt said suivi, didn't he? Well, now, what shall I do?

(ROSE comes in, dressed as she was, presumably, for the party.)

ROSE. *(as she enters)* Well, that little do of ours is hardly going to make history – I must say. Only nine o'clock, and not a bod left in the house. Not even the usual pair of drunks lying under the—

(Her voice trails away as she sees RON, who has turned from the table to face her.)

(Her voice a trifle shrill, but apparently controlled) Well, Ron. What a surprise.

RON. Hullo, Rose.

ROSE. I didn't see you at the party.

RON. I wasn't at the party. I missed it, I'm afraid.

KURT. Mona asked him, Rose.

MONA. I didn't – I promise I didn't, Rose.

ROSE. *(in control)* I really don't see that it matters who asked him. He's here, and I see that none of you has thought of giving the poor boy a drink. *(At the drink tray)* What's it to be, Ron? Still rosé?

RON. No. I don't drink these days.

ROSE. Don't you really? *(She picks up a bottle of brandy.)*

HETTIE. And nor do you, Rose – if you remember.

ROSE. *(putting back the bottle, after a pause)* No, nor I do. *(Approaching the table)* Well, how are you, Ron? You're looking very well. A bit thinner, perhaps—

RON. Yes. I am thinner. Settle a problem for me, will you? I have two hundred thousand francs here – the bank's run three times and Kurt suivied. Shall I give it?

ROSE. No. Take it in.

RON. That settles the problem nicely. All right, Kurt. Here we go. The fourth coup.

(He deals the cards. KURT takes his up, very slowly, trying to rattle RON. He makes a move to throw his cards face upwards – as if he had an eight or nine – and then holds them, laughing derisively.)

KURT. Card.

RON. So that's the sort of player you are, is it? Real old-fashioned funny stuff. I might have guessed it. *(He turns his cards up.)* Neuf en banque.

ROSE. Well done, Ron. Pay up, Kurt.

(KURT is doing so, trying to appear unconcerned.)

Don't worry, Ron. He won all this and more at the party.

RON. I'm not worrying.

ROSE. Why should you? *(To KURT)* Darling, shouldn't you be at your meeting?

KURT. Yes, I should. But I think I am waiting just a little longer – just to see our friend here safely out of the house. One is never knowing – with so much money on him – he could be being coshed or something.

RON. I won't have so much money on me.

(He is counting the notes. He removes twenty-five thousand and puts it in his breast pocket.)

Just what I came with – that's all.

(He wheels suddenly on **ROSE** *and thrusts out to her the bundle of remaining notes.)*

There you are. Take it.

ROSE. What are you talking about?

RON. Three seventy-five thousand. God knows it's not all I owe you – not by a long chalk – but you'll get the rest back one day – every bloody penny – with interest too. Meanwhile – take this to be going on with.

ROSE. Really, Ron. You mustn't be so hysterical.

RON. Take it, damn you. Take it.

(He screws the bills together and throws them at her. The bundle falls to the floor.)

Come on, Mona.

(He turns towards the steps left.)

KURT. Not quite so easily, my friend.

(He bars the way out, and then, as **RON** *stops, begins to walk slowly and menacingly towards him. Before he is there,* **RON**, *with a sudden gesture, has picked up a tumbler and broken it on a table. He holds the jagged edge towards* **KURT**.*)*

(Laughing) A tough little baby, I see. So much the more amusing—

(He picks up a heavy garden chair with one hand.)

It is good to see I am still being able to do that.

(He brings the other hand to the chair preparatory to using it as a weapon of offence.)

Now we shall see.

ROSE. *(quietly)* Kurt – if you touch him you'll never see me again as long as you live.

KURT. That is maybe a risk I am taking.

ROSE. It's no risk. It's a certainty. I don't lie when I say things like that.

RON. *(through his teeth, shivering slightly, his eyes on* **KURT**.*)* Only when you say things like I love you more than life.

ROSE. *(quietly)* That's right. Only when I say things like I love you more than life.

(She goes to **RON** *and gently takes the tumbler from his hand.* **KURT**, *meanwhile, has lowered the chair.)*

(Pointing to the money) Now pick that up.

RON. I'm not going to take it.

ROSE. I didn't say you were. I said pick it up.

(After a pause he stoops and gathers the bills. Then he hands them to her again.)

Put it on the table.

*(***RON** *does so.)*

If you like to tell me the name of your favourite charity, I'll send it to them in your name. Otherwise I'll send it to mine.

(He stands undecided, staring at her – wanting to say more, dissatisfied with the result of his scene, wanting to begin it again, but not knowing how. **ROSE** *smiles suddenly at him.)*

(Gently) You silly little boy.

(With a half-sob he turns and runs out left.)

(Urgently) See he's all right, Mona. Stay with him if you can. I know these moods. Anything can happen.

MONA. I'll do my best. I can't say I care for the thought of having a high hysteric on my hands. Still, I'll try.

ROSE. He's not so hard to handle. He just needs a little – looking after, that's all.

MONA. O.K. Well, good night. And sorry, too, I guess. Not really my fault though.

(She follows RON *out.* ROSE *suddenly collapses into a chair.* HETTIE *approaches her solicitously.)*

HETTIE. Back to bed, maybe?

ROSE. Certainly not. I've just come from bed and I feel fine. *(She laughs.)* What about that, eh? I bet he's been working that one out for months. Poor little beast. I suppose he meant to do it with just a couple of mille, which would have been just as good as a gesture, and wouldn't have been nearly so expensive. Winning all that money from Kurt must have gone to his head. Think how awful he'll feel in the morning when he remembers what he's given to charity – three seventy-five. Think how many sports jackets he could have bought himself for that.

(She is talking rapidly and a shade hysterically. HETTIE *is watching her with concern,* KURT *with a certain anger.)*

HETTIE. I think a little rest upstairs, don't you?

ROSE. Don't be such a bore, Hettie. *(Pointing to the money)* Listen, tomorrow when you're clearing up and after we're safely on our way to Switzerland, pop that in an envelope, and leave it for him at his stage door. He's dancing at the Théâtre du Casino Municipale—

KURT. How are you knowing that, my dear?

ROSE. I happened to see it in the local paper.

KURT. Yes. You are always no doubt looking in the local paper to see what is playing in the Théâtre du Casino Municipale.

ROSE. *(after a pause)* I haven't been down there to see him, you know – if that's what that rather heavy Teutonic irony implied.

KURT. You haven't been down, but you were maybe tempted to go – possibly?

ROSE. Maybe. Possibly. I haven't seen him dance often, and always enjoyed it when I have. He's very good and so is the company—

KURT. And why were you saying to me – don't touch him – don't touch him – but not to him are you saying much? It is all right for him to be pushing broken glass in my face, I am noticing—

ROSE. *(after a faint pause, battling with her anger)* Women's sympathies are usually with the underdog – Englishwomen especially. We're sentimental, you see.

KURT. Not too sentimental, I am hoping.

ROSE. *(rising, now angry)* Kurt, if you're out to make a scene you may get one – with warhead attached. Ron isn't the only hysteric in the world. Given the right mood, I can do all right too, you know. And I've *got* the right mood.

KURT. It is a good thing you are going to this sanatorium. A very good thing—

ROSE. Yes, it is. Go to your conference.

*(**KURT** nods and goes to the steps left.)*

KURT. Get them to make something light for me when I come back. Say, about an hour—

ROSE. No.

KURT. No?

ROSE. Unless you want to have supper alone, or with Hettie, if she'll join you. I'm going to bed.

KURT. A moment ago you were saying you are feeling fine – you are not wanting to go to bed—

ROSE. *(raising her voice)* I've changed my mind.

KURT. We will have a little supper together in your room.

ROSE. No.

KURT. Why not?

(Pause)

I am wanting to know why not?

ROSE. *(wearily)* Oh because I'm going down to the Théâtre du Casino Municipale, of course – to see Ron and take him out on the town and to beg him to come back to me. Oh Kurt! How can you be so damn stupid. The doctors have forbidden me this coast for the rest of my life, so I can never, never, never see him again – even if I wanted to. And do you think I want to? Do you really think I want to, Kurt? Do you think I enjoyed seeing him tonight?

KURT. It is not just a question of a girl to be seeing someone to be making a man jealous, my dear. There is too a question of feeling. Why are you feeling always so much for this boy?

ROSE. Put that in the past tense, and I might answer you,

KURT. *(advancing on her angrily)* I am not putting it in the past tense. I am putting it in the now tense.

ROSE. Present tense.

KURT. *(shouting)* Why are you still feeling so much for the boy – right now?

ROSE. *(shrugging)* Hangover.

KURT. Hangovers get cured.

ROSE. Yes. In time. So will this.

KURT. Himmel, you have had three months—

ROSE. The textbooks on emotional disorders give six, I believe – for complete recovery. *(She pats his hand.)* Don't worry, Kurt. After the sanatorium I shall have a clean bill of health. Go to your bankers.

(**KURT** *kisses her roughly. She accepts the embrace impassively. Then he turns and goes to the steps left.)*

See you tomorrow.

KURT. *(for once rather forlorn)* Why are you never feeling for me what you are feeling for this gigolo?

ROSE: One day, perhaps I will, Kurt. You may have to lose all your money, first, and pawn my jewels, and cry on my shoulder and need my help. Still, that could happen, I suppose.

KURT. My father was right when he is saying – never get involved with women. They are all crazy idiots, and about life are they knowing from nothing. From nothing.

*(He goes out. **ROSE** sits down wearily.)*

HETTIE. I hope he doesn't take you too seriously, and let those Swiss bankers get the better of him.

ROSE. Can you see him?

HETTIE. Frankly, I can't.

*(**ROSE** holds out her hand to **HETTIE**, who takes it.)*

ROSE. Do I have to marry him, Hettie?

HETTIE. Yes, dear. Quite frankly, you do.

ROSE. Otherwise, no lolly?

HETTIE. No lolly at all.

ROSE. If I sold this damn house—

HETTIE. It's been up for sale for five months. I haven't heard of an offer yet.

ROSE. In the Ron days I was going to live on the income from the sale – do you remember?

HETTIE. I remember.

ROSE. I was on the level, you know. I really did think someone would want to buy it.

HETTIE. You couldn't have given it away. I knew that.

ROSE. So I'd only have had the pictures to sell. And the car.

HETTIE. For what you could get.

ROSE. *(with a faint laugh)* Yes. Yes, it'd have been love in a cottage, all right. A smaller cottage than I'd even bargained for.

HETTIE. Or than *he'd* bargained for.

ROSE. *(looking up at her, gently)* Quite right, Hettie. You must always say things like that. Go on being an antidote, will you?

HETTIE. The strongest in the business. *(She turns away.)* I'm having a beer.

ROSE. *(murmuring)* The little twirp. Throwing money in my face, yet. Hm! I, bet he's making a lovely story of it now – down in the theatre, with all the chorus boys—

HETTIE. *(at drink tray)* And girls—

ROSE. Yes. And girls. *(Imitating* **RON***)* 'I showed her what I thought of her, all right. I showed her she couldn't treat me like a common little pick-up.' *(Excitedly)* No. Wait a minute. Down at the theatre he uses his accent, doesn't he? *(Imitating, again, with phoney Russian accent)* 'So. I draw myself up to my full height and I say – Madame – I pray you to accept this insignificant sum and present it, Madame, to any charity. *(Her voice trails away.)* Any charity.' *(With suppressed tears)* Oh, Hettie—

*(***HETTIE*** comes over and takes her hand again.)*

What an awful mess I've made of it all.

HETTIE. No dear. He's out of your life.

ROSE. *(angrily)* I didn't mean *him*. I meant me. I meant Kurt – I meant my whole damned existence. How the hell did I start it all? I can't even remember now. I know I loathed home – but a lot of girls do that. I know I read a lot of magazine trash about rich peers marrying humble working girls, and about the glittering, glamorous life of the international set, but a lot of girls do that too. I know I preferred Cannes to Edgbaston, and Florida to the Welfare State, but am I alone in that?

HETTIE. No, dear. I wouldn't say so.

ROSE. Then why is it me who's got to marry Kurt in three months' time?

HETTIE. Poor little multi-millionairess.

*(Pause. ***ROSE*** looks up at her and smiles.)*

ROSE. *(brusquely)* Quite right, Hettie. Self-pity – maudlin and ridiculous. As you never stopped saying to me once, I've made my bed and a very comfortable bed it's been too, and after Kurt – let me tell you, it's damn well going to be the most comfortable bed in Europe.

No one will ever have seen such a bed. It'll have
flounces and canopies and solid gold cherubs – and—

(She stops abruptly. RON *has come back on to the
terrace.)*

(Her voice level) I thought you went with Mona.

RON. Just to the end of the drive. I waited there till I saw
Kurt go.

ROSE. Very wise. What have you come back for? Your
money?

RON. *(murmuring)* No.

ROSE. It's over there, if you want it.

RON. I don't want it. I want you to have it.

ROSE. Yes. You made that clear just now. What have you
come back for then?

RON. To ask you to forgive me.

ROSE. All right. I've forgiven you. Now how are you going
to get back to Cannes?

RON. I hadn't thought.

ROSE. Hettie, would you ring up for a taxi? From the
Carlton. My account.

HETTIE. Right.

(She goes out.)

RON. *(after a pause, in a low voice)* Why do you hate me so
much?

ROSE. Do I hate you, Ron?

RON. You must. If you don't, then why do you say things
like 'have you come back for your money', and 'my
account'? They're only meant to hurt, aren't they?

ROSE. Yes, I suppose that's how they must seem.

RON. Surely if either of us is to hate the other, it ought to
be me hating you – oughtn't it?

ROSE. Yes. It ought.

RON. Oh God, Rose, how could you do that to me? What
did I do to you to make you do that?

ROSE. You did nothing, Ron.

RON. I must have done something. Every night I've tried to think – what could it have been. What the hell could it possibly have been. *(After a pause)* Was it that pullover I ordered without telling you—?

ROSE. No, Ron. It wasn't the pullover.

RON. Something I said, then. That row we had in the Martinez?

ROSE. No. It wasn't the row in the Martinez.

RON. It must have been something. I think I've been over everything I said or did that week a hundred times – and I still don't know. I still don't know, Rose. Are you sure it wasn't the pullover?

ROSE. I'm sure it wasn't the pullover.

RON. What was it then?

ROSE. I'd just stopped loving you, Ron – that's all.

RON. You wouldn't – like that. Not unless I'd done something really bad. I know that.

ROSE. How do you know?

RON. I know you.

ROSE. Perhaps you don't. Perhaps you never did.

RON. I did, anyway. Knew you like the back of my hand. If I hadn't I wouldn't have felt about you the way I did.

ROSE. How was that, Ron?

RON. Well – happy – and – well, you know – safe—

ROSE. Yes. I know.

RON. No. It must have been something awful I did—

ROSE. *(explosively)* Oh God, why can't you grow up? Must you go on through life thinking that everything bad that ever happens to you must always be your own fault? I just stopped loving you. There wasn't any reason. I just stopped loving you. It happens, you know. It happens every day—

(**HETTIE** *comes out of the house.*)

HETTIE. The taxi's on its way.

ROSE. Thank you, Hettie.

HETTIE. And Fiona's boy friend's arrived to take her down to the Ciel et Enfer. She's waiting in the hall to say goodbye.

ROSE. *(with sudden violence)* I'm not going to—

HETTIE. *(bewildered)* I thought she'd better not come out here. But if you want—

ROSE. No. I don't want her out here. I just don't want to say goodbye to Fiona. Get it?

HETTIE. Yes.

ROSE. Why should I have my feelings bulldozed by that self-contained little snow-maiden, and be always expected to come up with a happy maternal smile: 'Well, good-bye, Fiona, darling. So glad you've enjoyed your stay. Write to me, won't you, and look after yourself – and remember Mummy will be thinking of you every day – even if you never spend one single damn second of the next three months thinking of Mummy.' I'm not going to do it, Hettie. I'm not going to.

HETTIE. Yes. I heard you. What shall I tell her?

ROSE. That I'm very, very tired, and that I'll call her at the airport.

HETTIE. Right.

(She goes out.)

RON. That's funny.

ROSE. What's funny?

RON. My feelings have been bulldozed all right – you can't deny it – but I come up smiling.

ROSE. I haven't noticed you smiling.

RON. That's just a figure of speech. I'm here, aren't I? – apologizing and eating dirt when I ought to be hating you and despising you – the way you do me. *(Angrily)* Why can't I hate you?

ROSE. Perhaps you haven't tried hard enough.

RON. Tried? Lord, I've tried. I'll go on trying too – never you fear. Only – *(his voice falters)* it doesn't seem much use – I don't know why.

(He turns away from her to hide his emotion.)

ROSE. *(her voice harsh with anger)* Don't cry – for God's sake – don't cry.

RON. *(quickly)* I wasn't. I'm quite all right. It was only just seeing you after all this time—

ROSE. *(her voice still harsh)* I prefer you in your money-throwing, glass-breaking mood—

RON. That was a give-away, wasn't it? You don't do that if you don't care. I was going to be all hard and bright and tough and couldn't care less tonight – the old Ron Vale – the one you met at the Casino that night – remember – and before you came out I wasn't doing too badly either – and then— *(He stops.)*

ROSE. And then?

RON. And then you did come out.

ROSE. *(still hard)* And something snapped, as they say in novels – and everything became a blur—

RON. You could put it like that, I suppose. *(Quickly)* God, you've changed, Rose. You were always a bit hard at times, I'm not denying – but nothing like this. It's not the way I'll be wanting to remember you.

ROSE. But it's the way you should remember me. It might help you to hate me—

RON. *(sadly)* No, it won't. I know it won't. I suppose the truth is, if you need somebody enough it doesn't seem to matter that much what they do to you, or what they turn out to be. In spite of everything, you see – and I really am eating dirt now all right – I still want like mad to be in your life – only one of three hundred other guests, if you like, and on sufferance from that German bastard – but just to see you and talk to you now and then. *(Shamefacedly)* Fine bloody manly attitude that is, isn't it? Still, I can't help it. It's the truth and I thought you'd like to know it.

ROSE. *(now becoming desperate)* Why did you think I'd like to know it? Why?

RON. God, if I'd treated another girl the way you treated me, I wouldn't mind knowing she'd forgiven me.

ROSE. I don't want to know it, Ron. I'd far rather think you hadn't forgiven me and never would. I'd far rather think you had some guts.

RON. Well, I haven't and I've admitted it. *(After a pause)* Maybe I shouldn't have told you then. Only when you've got certain feelings about someone, it's damned hard to stop yourself saying it.

ROSE. *(facing him squarely)* It's not hard at all, Ron. It's quite easy. And what feelings are you talking about? Are you trying to suggest – love? That *you* feel *love*?

RON. *(nodding, at length)* That's about it, I suppose.

ROSE. *(laughing)* That's not about it, Ron – it's nowhere within a hundred miles of it. Love means giving, doesn't it – and what have you ever done all your life except take – take anything from motor-cars to other people's love? *(Derisively.)* You feel love? That'll be the day.

RON. It doesn't matter much what you call it, does it? I've told you the truth.

ROSE. You haven't. You're just trying to sneak into my life again – through the servants' entrance, this time – not like that first night when you used the front door and you were oh so cocky and sure of yourself – and convinced no one could ever resist you – not even me – not even me—

RON. Yes. I was a bit cocky then, I grant. Seems I've changed a bit this summer—

ROSE. Oh my God! Isn't there anything in the world I can say to you that will make you angry?

(She turns quickly away. RON *stares at her, surprised.)*

RON. Do you want to make me angry?

ROSE. Of course I don't. I don't give a damn what you feel. Why should I? Why the hell should I?

(Her voice is beginning to betray her. **RON** *has taken a few faltering steps towards her, when* **HETTIE** *appears.)*

HETTIE. Taxi's here.

ROSE. *(murmuring)* Thank God.

*(***HETTIE** *stares at* **ROSE**'s *face as she stands, her back still to* **RON.** **ROSE** *signs her to go away.* **HETTIE** *turns abruptly and goes out. When* **ROSE** *faces* **RON** *again she has partly recovered herself. She picks up the money on the table.)*

You'd better take this. You'll be needing it.

*(***RON** *shakes his head quickly.* **ROSE** *throws the money back on to the table.)*

I'm afraid it won't be possible for us to meet again, Ron. You see, I'm going away to Switzerland tomorrow and won't be back here any more.

RON. I didn't know. Oh Lord! That's terrible, isn't it?

ROSE. Why terrible?

RON. For me, I meant. We've got a season soon in Paris. Perhaps—

ROSE. *(quickly)* Perhaps. *(Brightly)* How's the dancing going, Ron?

RON. Not bad. I'm going to try for the Garden next year.

ROSE. Good. I hope you make it.

RON. If I do, that might mean we could meet in London too. Or New York. They go there quite a bit.

ROSE. Yes, I know.

RON. *(quietly)* I'm not going to let you right out of my life, you know. You say I've got no guts – but about that I have. And I don't mind the servants' entrance. Hell. Why should I? It's where I belong.

ROSE. Why you more than me?

RON. You've made the grade: I haven't.

ROSE. Well, goodbye, Ron.

RON. Can't I stay on just a little bit longer?

ROSE. No. I'm sorry.

RON. I've nothing to do in town, except eat by myself somewhere and go to bed. Can't I stay on just a bit?

ROSE. No, I'm sorry. I've got some people coming in in a minute, you see, and—

RON. *(with a smile)* And you don't want them to meet common Ron. I see. All right. I'll go quietly. Goodbye. Or rather – be seeing you, Rose.

(He turns to the steps and then turns back.)

(In genuine bewilderment) I wish you'd tell me what it was I did to make you change like that. *(After a pause for thought)* Listen, was it anything to do with that day when you said I always stayed in the sea too long, and you were waving from the beach and I was on the raft pretending not to notice—?

*(**ROSE**'s expression, not unimpassive until now, suddenly dissolves completely. She puts her hands quickly to her face and turns away, but her tears have been all too visible to **RON**. He stares at her.)*

It was that, then?

*(**ROSE**, in tears, does not answer. **RON** walks slowly towards her.)*

ROSE. *(as she senses his closeness)* Go away. Oh, God, please go away.

RON. No. Not when you're like this. Was it that, Rose?

ROSE. *(with a wail)* No – it wasn't that. Of course it wasn't that—

RON. What's the matter, then?

ROSE. Nothing's the matter. I'm feeling tired – that's all. Get Hettie for me—

RON. No. I won't do that. *(He puts his hands on her shoulders.)*

ROSE. Please go away, Ron. Please.

RON. No. I won't do that either, now.

ROSE. Oh God. Ten more seconds. Ten more seconds, and it was done. Why did you say that about the beach?

(She turns to him, still crying, and holds him to her. Then she lets him raise her head with his hand and kiss her.)

RON. I thought it might really have been that.

ROSE. You damn little fool.

RON. Why have you been pretending to me?

ROSE. I haven't been pretending—

RON. *(still holding her)* Is there any point in fighting it any more?

ROSE. No. I suppose there isn't. I suppose there isn't.

*(She recovers herself. **RON** looks at her, frowning and puzzled.)*

RON. *(explosively)* But why? Why? Why those awful things you said to me on that machine? It wasn't just the money. I know that.

ROSE. How do you know that?

RON. I know my Rose better than most people. Better than Hettie or Kurt. Why? Why?

ROSE. Oh God, you're such a fool.

(She breaks away from him and takes a cigarette.)

Haven't you any idea?

(He shakes his head.)

No. I suppose it would be the very last idea that'd occur to you. It was for you, Ron.

RON. For me? And make me bloody miserable for three months—

ROSE. We weren't thinking so much of months, Ron. More of years. Many, many years. A lifetime, in fact.

RON. You said 'we'. You mean Hettie and you?

ROSE. Yes. Hettie and I.

RON. The interfering old—

ROSE. Don't blame *her,* Ron. It was *my* doing. Mine entirely.

RON. I don't get the idea, Rose.

ROSE. We thought – I thought – and I was right too, mind you – I thought if things hadn't lasted between us, it might have been worse for you than for me.

RON. Why?

ROSE. You might have been left a bit – stranded—

RON. Stranded? Me? Hell, I can take, care of myself.

ROSE. Cocky again, eh?

RON. I can, Rose. Really, I can. I mean, look at the way I've looked after myself since you did ditch me. Bloody lonely, I grant, and not sleeping or eating too well either. But doing all right, I tell you. Ask anyone in the Company. As a matter of fact I've been dancing better these last three months than ever before in my life—

ROSE. *(looking at him)* I'm glad to hear it.

RON. Oh, my God – what a damn crazy idea! Typical of a woman. And when you think what I've been going through since August. Of course you've been giving gay parties up here.

ROSE. The parties haven't been awfully gay, Ron. At least— not for me.

(Pause)

RON. Just torturing ourselves for no reason. No reason at all.

(He embraces her again.)

(At length) Going to give up Kurt?

(Pause)

ROSE. *(quietly, at length)* Yes.

RON. And marry me?

ROSE. No.

RON. Oh, yes you are, you know. Why do you think you're not?

ROSE. We haven't the money.

RON. *(laughing)* Money! *(He looks up at the house.)*

ROSE. No one will buy it, Ron.

RON. That's all right. We can live in it.

ROSE. *(after a pause)* Yes. I suppose we can.

RON. And with the money I get from the ballet we can pay for food and things. Or you might perhaps be able to get me something that pays a bit better.

ROSE. No. You must stick to dancing, Ron. Whatever happens, you must stick to that.

RON. Well, anyway – we'll live.

ROSE. Yes.

(**RON** *has wandered to the drink tray.*)

RON. We must have a toast on this, don't you think? Or are you really on the level about the wagon?

ROSE. No, of course not. When have you ever known me on the level about the wagon?

RON. Brandy and soda?

ROSE. And not too light on the brandy, either. *(Approaching him)* I think perhaps we'd better wait a little bit about getting married, Ron.

RON. How long?

ROSE. Oh – only – say a couple of months. Not much longer.

RON. Why?

ROSE. Well – one thing – it might be nice to get married after the winter—

RON. Very charming and sentimental idea, considering who it's from. Have all your marriages been in the spring?

ROSE. *(smiling)* This is a very special one.

RON. Granted. *(He raises his glass.)* Well – to the spring.

ROSE. *(murmuring)* To the spring.

RON. And to no more practical jokes, that make me wish I'd never been born – even if they *are* for my good.

ROSE. Oh, Ron—

RON. And no more tears either. We've done with that, now.

ROSE. People can cry from just being glad, you know—

RON. *(stroking her hair)* Yes, and later tonight it's quite likely I'll be doing that, too. But when we're together from now on – let's try and keep it smiles. Smiles all the way.

ROSE. I'll try. And I'll succeed too. Because it won't be hard at all.

RON. It's funny about us, isn't it? I mean, both of us coming from the same town, both of us knowing exactly what we want – and exactly how we're going to get it, too – and then, suddenly, what have we got? Just what everybody else in the world has got – each other. Whoever it is that fixes things up there has quite a line in practical jokes himself – you've got to grant—

ROSE. *(smiling tenderly at him)* Yes, Ron. In the past I haven't always granted the accuracy of your observations on the Universe and its meaning – but oddly enough, that one I do.

(There is a raucous sound from the drive.)

TAXI-DRIVER. *(off)* Mais, dites-donc. Qu'est ce qui a? On va attendre toute la nuit, ou quoi?

RON. *(calling down)* On vient tout de suite. *(Turning back)* Shall I send him away, or shall we take it together, and have a night on the town?

ROSE. A night on the town, of course.

RON. *(doubtfully)* Good. But you know we can't exactly afford one of *your* sort of nights—

ROSE. Why not? Look what we've got, Ron. *(She picks up the money from the table.)* And what's left over after our orgy I'll put on red. Yes. It's red tonight. It'll come up ten times running, and all our troubles will be over. Let's go.

RON. Hadn't you better have a coat? It gets a bit chilly these nights—

ROSE. Yes. I suppose it does. Get me my camel hair, would you? You know the one?

(**RON** *nods.*)

It's in my cupboard upstairs.

RON. O.K.

ROSE. And as you go tell Hettie to stop listening at the window and come out.

(**RON** *nods, smiles at her and goes.* **ROSE** *takes a long gulp from her brandy, and then begins to cough violently.* **HETTIE** *comes out.*)

(*Between coughs*) There's not a damn thing in the world you can do about it.

HETTIE. Oh yes, there is. I can tell him about the sanatorium.

ROSE. I'll tell him different. It's me he'll believe, because he'll want to. You're the enemy.

HETTIE. I'll get the doctors to fight it.

ROSE. (*shrugging*) Oh God, Hettie. I've fought doctors all my life, and I've always won.

HETTIE. (*fiercely*) I'll get the doctors to tell *him* exactly what a winter in this place must mean for you. That he'll have to believe.

ROSE. Why? He knows that doctors can be wrong. So do you. So do I. They've been wrong about me often enough before. Why not now?

HETTIE. This time you know they're not.

ROSE. I don't think I know anything very much, any more, Hettie. Nor does he. I think you'll find he'll be just as content as I am to put it all on red. That's not such a bad way to gamble, you know. Systems don't always pay off, and who am I saying *that* to?

(*She turns and smiles at* **HETTIE** *tenderly.*)

You won't leave me this time, will you? Not, at least, until after the winter—

HETTIE. *(suddenly losing all her toughness: a broken, bewildered old woman)* Oh God, Rose. You know there's no gamble in this. You know it as well as I do. It's a certainty.

(ROSE merely smiles.)

But why? Why? Why?

ROSE. *(Echoing what she once said to Ron.)* Why not?

(She looks tenderly at HETTIE'S distressed face.)

I've picked up the hand, Hettie. I can't refuse to play the cards, can I?

HETTIE. Of course you can, when playing them must mean—

(She stops.)

ROSE. *(gently)* I lose the game? Would you do that, Hettie? Would you be proud of yourself if you did? Oh no, surely we've got to play the rules, haven't we? I can't claim I don't know them, either. I learnt them at my father's knee. Quite often, in his few sober moments, he used to say to me: 'If there's one thing that's certain in this world, Rose, my girl, it's that you'll come to a bad end.' I believed him, too, and always have. Only, being a bit of a puritan myself, as you know, I'd always imagined an end far more lurid and horrifying than a winter in Cannes with a man I love more than life. More than life? Silly phrase, that – isn't it? Just a woman's exaggeration.

(HETTIE is crying.)

ROSE. Oh, Hettie – please.

(RON comes back with ROSE's coat, brushes past HETTIE without looking at her, and helps ROSE into the coat.)

Thank you, Ron. I was just talking about you.

RON. *(embarrassed before HETTIE)* Nicely?

ROSE. Yes. I think even *your* vanity would be satisfied.

(She hands him the money she has been holding.)

You'd better take this, and cause a sensation at Maxim's by being seen paying for me for once.

RON. That's right. Back to normal. Needling poor old Ron again. Hell, have you forgotten it's my money?

ROSE. You gave it to me.

RON. Yes, but I won it.

ROSE. Yes. You won it – and gave it to me. *(She smiles at his angry face.)* Oh, well, it couldn't matter less, could it? From now on, what's mine is yours, anyway.

(She turns to look at **HETTIE** *who is crying. She walks over to her and puts her hands on her shoulders.)*

(With a smile) Hettie. Hettie – for heaven's sake. I'm terribly happy.

(She kisses her gently on the cheek and then goes to **RON**. *She takes a red rose from a vase and puts it in his buttonhole.)*

It's a bit early for Maxim's. Let's have dinner at that new place on the port, and then try a bar that Mona told me about the other day – somewhere on the Rue d'Antibes – tout ce qu'il y a de plus hellish, I'm sure, but worth a try. It's called the Chien something—

(They begin to go down the steps together.)

RON. Yes. I know it. The Chien Noir—

ROSE. Noir? Oh dear. I hope that isn't an omen. Anyway it doesn't matter. I've said rouge and rouge is what I mean. After that – well, I suppose what we could do is—

(They have disappeared. **HETTIE** *makes a hopeless gesture after* **ROSE**, *but she has not looked back.)*

(Curtain)

End of Play

MUSIC USE NOTE

Licensees are solely responsible for obtaining formal written permission from copyright owners to use copyrighted music in the performance of this play and are strongly cautioned to do so. If no such permission is obtained by the licensee, then the licensee must use only original music that the licensee owns and controls. Licensees are solely responsible and liable for all music clearances and shall indemnify the copyright owners of the play(s) and their licensing agent, Samuel French, against any costs, expenses, losses and liabilities arising from the use of music by licensees. Please contact the appropriate music licensing authority in your territory for the rights to any incidental music.

IMPORTANT BILLING AND CREDIT REQUIREMENTS

If you have obtained performance rights to this title, please refer to your licensing agreement for important billing and credit requirements.

Lightning Source UK Ltd.
Milton Keynes UK
UKOW05f1452210814

237319UK00007B/79/P